Praise

How to Create a $1,000,000 Speech

"For decades I have watched Judith Briles build and sustain a successful speaking career while authoring more books than most people read. Once Judith started helping others write books that were worth reading, she opened a new chapter of her life, which her talents are ideally suited for: How to be a successful speaker.

Judith is not selling a get-rich-quick promise— more a logical, practical, sustainable approach. By learning from those who have mastered the skills you are looking for will save you time and resources. Learning from Judith Briles could well be your best purchase of the year."

— Patricia Fripp, CSP, CPAE - Past President, National Speakers Association

"BRAVA! BRAVA! What an incredible book. My copy is tagged, noted, and circled throughout. Fantastic resources!

What you are holding in your hands is the epic accumulation of 40+ years of expertise in the publishing industry. A virtual 'Wonka's Golden Ticket,' this book opens the vault with full-color examples, contracts, checklists, and a level of expert advice that few books on the subject matter offer."

— Jeffrey Keen, President & CEO
of American Book Fest

———————

"The best place to sell yourself, your product, service, or idea is from the platform. Judith Briles reveals in this succinct treasure of a book the exact steps of how an aspiring or even seasoned speaker can create a speech that is both impactful AND extraordinarily profitable."

— Daniel Hall, Host of the
RealFastResults.com podcast

"OMG ... The book is FABulous!

If you have ever wanted to turn your book or your life into a Million Dollar Speaking career, you MUST buy Judith Briles' *How to Create a $1,000,000 Speech*! Judith Briles' candor, content, strategies, and tips are a blueprint for speaking success. A successful *New York Times* bestselling author, the genius behind AuthorYOU and an in-demand speaker, Judith hasn't 'studied' the process, she has lived it.

In this book, she shares how she turned her nightmare into a flourishing speaking success and walks you through the journey so you can do it, too. I wish I had *How to Create a $1,000,000 Speech* when I started my speaking career!"

— Susan RoAne
Keynote Speaker, Networking Coach
and author of *How to Work a Room*®
and *Secrets of Savvy Networking*

"My number one way to sell books (from my *1001 Ways to Market Your Books*) is speaking. All the bestselling authors of books on spirituality, self-help, fiction, poetry, business, relationships, romance, and children's books, use speaking as their primary way to sell books.

You can, too! If you want to make money as a speaker AND sell a lot more books, read *How to Create a $1,000,000 Speech*."

—John Kremer, author,
1001 Ways to Market Your Books

———————

"Speaking is the best marketing strategy for creating a million dollar business. Dr. Judith Briles shows how thought leaders can take their ideas and turn them into dollars."

— Dan Janal, author,
Write Your Book in a Flash!

"Most authors are leaving thousands of dollars on the table by not speaking in front of audiences. Don't you be one of them. *How to Create a $1,000,000 Speech* explains in step-by-step detail how to start cashing in on a lucrative revenue stream via public speaking.

Judith Briles, a superwoman in the author and publishing world, has made triple that amount through good, old-fashioned marketing, storytelling that audiences love and knowing exactly how to get through to the decision-makers who can hire her.

In this, her 36th book, Judith pulls back the curtain on how to follow in her footsteps, regardless of your topic or genre. Must reading, even for shy timid introverts."

— Joan Stewart
The Publicity Hound
PublicityHound.com

"Selling books at the back of the room can be a lucrative way to sell books. But you have to get the speaking contract first. Judith Briles is the acknowledged expert in doing both, and she demonstrates that here. I just can't believe she gives away all her secrets!"

— Brian Jud, Executive Director of the Association of Publishers for Special Sales, and author, *Beyond the Bookstore* and *How to Make Real Money Selling Books*

———————

"Anyone familiar with Dr. Judith Briles knows she is also an exceptional cook. In her latest addition to the *AuthorYOU Mini-Guide Series*, *How to Create a $1,000,000 Speech*, she dishes up a five-course meal on everything you'll ever need to make yourself a successful speaker.

All the ingredients are here: the costs of speaking, finding your niche, branding yourself effectively, crafting your speech, finding sponsors, marketing yourself—all topped off with her 40+ years of being a bestselling author and sought-after speaker.

Keep your highlighter in hand—you'll be making note after note—to replicate this recipe for success. Bon Appétit!"

— Nick Zelinger,
Award-winning book designer
NZGraphics.com

DR. JUDITH BRILES

How to Create a
$1,000,000
Speech

The Award-Winning AuthorYOU Mini-Guide Series

Mile High Press, Ltd.
www.MileHighPress.com
MileHighPress@aol.com
303-885-2207

MileHigh Press

Books may be purchased in quantity
by contacting the publisher directly:
Mile High Press, Ltd., PO Box 460880,
Aurora, CO 80046 or by calling 303-885-2207.

Editing: John Maling, EditingByJohn@aol.com
Cover and Interior Design: Nick Zelinger, NZGraphics.com
Illustrations: Don Sidle, www.DonSidle.com

978-1885331670 (paper)
978-1885331687 (ebook)
978-1885331670 (audiobook)
LCCN: 20189328263

Business | Public Speaking | Communications

First Edition   Printed in the United States

For speakers who desire to become seriously successful:

When you speak, you have the opportunity to deliver a miracle with your words.

Those who hear you can experience a different world; and view their life differently.

What an opportunity. What a responsibility. Your audiences will thank you.

CONTENTS

PART 3: READY ... SET ... GO

Foreword

What you are holding in your hands is the epic accumulation of over 40 years of expertise in the publishing industry. A virtual "Wonka's Golden Ticket," this book opens the vault with full color examples, contracts, checklists, and a level of expert advice that few books on the subject matter offer.

Judith Briles is a Publishing Warrior! She has lived it and now she puts it all out on the line in this book. She has made a career with her speaking and publishing, earning over $3,000,000 in speaking fees and selling over $2,000,000 in books, accomplishing a level of success that any speaker or author would aspire to.

I've had the pleasure of knowing Judith for over 10 years and in that time she has always been a fierce advocate for authors and their continuing success.

One of the main reasons why I've always been on the same wavelength with Judith is, like her, I view all business acts through the prism of marketing and publicity. How is this media coverage, book, book award, or speaking engagement going to further the author's career, expand his/her platform, and create the foundation for an author's next project?

Part of the journey to success as an author or speaker, is being able to attract and learn from established mentors in the industry. There are many out there that set up shop and claim to know everything there is to know about how to be successful as an author, yet deliver platitudes and surface information you could learn from any blog or internet search. The real experts, like Judith, hold the keys to success through living it, learning, growing, and expanding their expertise. Real mentors DEEP DIVE beyond the surface and share the road signs to success as well as how to avoid the potholes and detours that might appear in your path.

I've been an executive in the publishing industry for over 20 years, and I can unequivocally state that my early career would have been a whole lot smoother if I had had this book in my hands!

Judith's work as a book shepherd is unmatchable in the industry. The excellence of both her and her client's publications have been some of the most professional books that have come across our editorial desk.

Never doubt yourself! Live your passion and be in it for the long haul. I promise you, being an author and expert speaker will be a rewarding and satisfying endeavor.

Join Judith on this journey to your success and change the landscape of your professional life!

To Your Continued Success,

Jeffrey Keen
President & CEO
American Book Fest

The 15th Annual Best Book Awards
www.AmericanBookFest.com
March 2018

The first hint that I would become a speaker started in the third grade–I always got dings on my report card from my teacher. I was 8 years old and a motormouth in the classroom. Who would have known at that time, people would pay to hear and read my words when I grew up!

Part 1:
In the Beginning

Life-changing speeches
can start with a question.
"Why speak?" is one of them.

1

Why Speak?

Because ...

The public and a specific sector needs and wants your message, your smarts, your expertise.

Because ...

You can solve problems and provide answers that a group or an individual needs.

Because ...

You can meet amazing people.

Because ...

You can go places you never imagined.

Because ...

It can be enormously fun and exciting.

Because ...

You can sell a lot of books.

You can make money with your ideas, with the words that spill out of your mouth.

Welcome to my world.

One that I have lived in for 40 years.

How cool are these reasons? Very cool, I think. As a speaker, you make a difference. Whether as a problem solver or an entertainer, being a speaker is something that was never on my dance card growing up—although, I confess, I always got in trouble in elementary school for talking too much. For me, it was an evolution. I had information. I had something to say. And I discovered that there were many who wanted, in fact needed, to hear what I had to say ... and what I wrote in my books.

> *The fear of public speaking is known as glossophobia.*

Welcome to the Minority!

Approximately 10 percent of any given population loves speaking to a group—just about any group. They have little to no fear and get a huge buzz speaking in front of a large crowd—but the size of the gathering doesn't matter.

Yet, there is another 10 percent of any given population who are genuinely terrified of public speaking, literally. This group can become physically debilitated with even the thought of standing up in front of people.

The fear of public speaking is known as glossophobia. And, then there are those in between—anywhere from 74 to 80 percent of the general population has some form of speech anxiety. Yikes—that's a huge percentage. No wonder when speakers get on a stage and deliver their message, so many are in awe of what they do. When you make the decision to become a speaker, you are in a distinct minority. And, as a minority member—with practice and expertise—you can win the prize: repeat business!

> *Someone is in the audience that desperately needs to be there and hear you.*

The roughly 80 percent of you can join the 10 percent who view getting in front of a crowd with a microphone in hand as "dessert." All you need is desire, a group to speak to, and practice. Sure, you will have butterflies and a few nerves. It will pass.

And the outcome, when it's over? Think simply wonderful.

- First, you did it.

- Second, you shared information you were invited to deliver.

- And third, there may be someone in the audience that desperately needs to be there and hear you. Your words can become a tipping point for change.

That's huge … and if you got paid—terrific. And if you sold books, it's a bonus! Welcome to my world—one that I have lived in for 40 years.

Everyone has a story.
What's yours?
It could be the seeding
of your first speech ...
or show up in a later one.

2

How I Became a Full-Time Professional Speaker ...
My Story and Building My Platform

*Little did I know that losing everything
material would seed my future niche.*

Picture this: You have an idea for a book that is
rejected by every major publisher, a book that
contains extensive research and interviews.
You know it has merit. You can feel it in every
bone of your body. You know that it's a breakout
opportunity ... and could leapfrog your speaking
career and be a potential best seller. Do you
scrap it ... or do you keep pushing because in
your heart of hearts you know it's big?

That's where I was in the '70s as a stockbroker for EF Hutton. I had been teaching my Financial Savvy for Women and Financial Savvy for Couples workshops for several years at a community college. ***Sold out each time, there had be more.*** Oh, I know—a book. I knew zip about writing a book so I hired a tutor to show me how. In 1981, *The Woman's Guide to Financial Savvy* was birthed, landing me on *Good Morning America* and requests for me to speak started to come in from around the country.

It led to other book deals and then I was blind-sided financially. The same year I published my bestselling financial book for women, I was taken down by another woman—a close friend and a partner. Few knew how devastating my financial hit was until I published *Woman to Woman: From Sabotage to Support* in 1987.

Now, picture this: It's late 1986—I have just come through an embezzlement that personally cost me in excess of one million dollars, a health crisis, and a challenge to my company. I had an idea ... I had completed the work for my dissertation on why women undermine other women; had completed some 300 one-on-one interviews with women; and had begun writing the commercial book ... a book on the topic I was personally immersed in, quite painfully.

> *Little did I know that losing*
> *everything material in my life*
> *would seed my future niche.*

The topic was one I was passionate about. I had a vision for the path it would take me on. I was committed in time, energy, and money to make it happen. It was the 28 rejections from New York publishers that created a bit of a roadblock along the way. Everything from, "It doesn't fit our list," to "No media will ever cover this type of topic," to feminist Gloria Steinem telling me, "Don't write about this ... don't publish this," over dinner one evening at a conference we were both speaking at in Milwaukee.

"But Gloria, *Ms.* magazine went under because of the backstabbing and undermining of your female staff ...," I responded.

She didn't want to really delve into what was going on at *Ms.* What she did say was, "If you publish this, you will give them (the men) more information to use against us (we women)."

I noodled on her words and chose to go forward. After all, how can you fix anything if you continue to bury it? That topic was women and sabotage, or specifically, why women undermine other women and how to change it. A taboo topic ... one that no one was speaking on and certainly no one was writing about. A topic I knew plenty about after just going through embezzlement where my female partner had stolen money from a construction loan that I had personally guaranteed. And I had gone back and earned my doctorate in business administration. The topic: Ethics: Do Women Undermine Other Women?

Not knowing a lick about self-publishing (outside of it meaning vanity press and taboo for "legit" authors), I sold the book to a small New York press, ignoring the advice of all. My agent told me to ... he believed in the book as well.

Because I was already speaking on financial issues, being in front of a crowd wasn't a problem. I had important information. What I quickly discovered was that I was not alone. Women were approaching me about being "betrayed" by another woman. Everything in my body told me that there was a demand for my topic—ahhh, speaking engagements?

Your Speaking and Book Platforms

If you plan to write a book, use it for marketing your speaking expertise. I had a Platform in the '80s. It just wasn't called that back then. You need a Platform.

> *There is nothing accidental about creating your Platform. All successful businesses, speakers, experts, and authors have one. Their success and survival depend on it.*

The Platform consists of three key areas: ***Vision, Passion,*** and ***Commitment.*** Think of it as a funnel with three balls. Each is connected to the author as they flow through the neck. While in the funnel, they are tossed about as your book and speech are getting ready for birth. Then there is a fourth area that comes into play—***People***. They will find you through your channels of *Vision, Passion,* and *Commitment.*

When the internet blossomed, many believed that the Platform was all about the people you were connected with. Granted, you've got to have people to listen to you and buy your books, but the three factors of *Vision, Passion,* and *Commitment* are essential. People won't care about you or your book or any presentation you want to give if you don't have these.

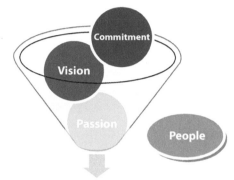

Author and Book Platforms

The Vision Factor

It starts with **Vision**—what you (the author) visualize and feel is the big picture. Within your *Vision*, your ideas formulate, they take root and embrace all the "what-ifs" that can come your way. Where do you see your book taking you? Where do you see taking your book? What about speaking? What type of groups do you imagine speaking to? What kind of problems and pain do they have? What groups do they belong to? Who is your audience? If you think "everyone," you will get lost in the crowd. Creating a niche is powerful, so narrow who your book is for. Go where a smaller crowd can find you as you reach out as the expert/the go-to person.

When *Woman to Woman: From Sabotage to Support* was initially published in 1987, I thought it was for every working woman. I was so wrong. No book is for everyone. The belief that it was came from naiveté on my part. It was part of my *Vision*. Yet I knew there was a problem. I understood what the emotional, physical, and financial effects were for the working woman. Therefore, I thought that all working women would see my *Vision*. Wrong!

I thought it was ideal for the general workplace. Wrong again. Was corporate America scared to death of the topic—women undermining women? You've got to be kidding! I had conducted a national study that included several thousand men and women; interviewed and listened to hundreds of painful stories of betrayal; and discovered that productivity and turnover were directly related. Surely corporate America was ready for this message. I was wrong, wrong, wrong. Women undermining and harassing other women was a hot potato. Gender harassment topics were forbidden. Sexual harassment topics, though—men harassing women—were in.

My *Vision* was that the mainstream media would embrace it. I was right. *Oprah* loved it. So did *CNN, Donahue, Sally, Geraldo* and every other first-name host along with the *Wall Street Journal, People* magazine, *Time, Newsweek, USA Today*, local press, radio, and TV across the country, even the *National Enquirer. Woman to Woman* was a publicist's dream.

After the first *Oprah* appearance, my office received a call from business expert Tom Peters' personal assistant. She had heard about the book and knew I had just been on *Oprah*.

The women in his office were driving him nuts with the backstabbing and gossiping. Could I come in and talk with them ... and bring a copy of the *Oprah* show? I did. Not surprisingly, he was leery of the topic—the hot-potato factor— and too hot for the corporate workplace for him to openly endorse ... but would I help with his office problem?

I Found My Niche!

It wasn't until several Directors of Nursing heard me speak on the topic that I found the "right" corporate workplace. My niche was going to be the female-dominated healthcare workplace. The field of nursing was a viper's den of undermining and toxicity. The first book specifically for health care, *The Briles Report on Women in Health Care*, was birthed in 2003 and became the main selection for the Nurses Book Society and was its best seller. Later books on the topic were specifically written for the healthcare field with the latest in 2009:

Stabotage! How to Deal with the Pit Bulls, Skunks, Snakes, Scorpions and Slugs in the Health Care Workplace (revised 2013). Speaking requests and book sales skyrocketed.

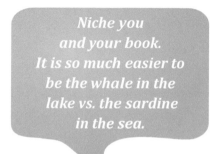

Niche you and your book. It is so much easier to be the whale in the lake vs. the sardine in the sea.

Your *Vision* creates the big picture—I took my book on major shows and it was covered by the media. It was the first book with a national study of the topic. I could see it used within the corporate workplace. But the right workplace had to be discovered. It was. I saw it branding me and my speaking. My controversial expertise was discovered by a market I hadn't thought about before. And, it took me to the next level of speaking. I sold my business. I wanted out of California. I transitioned into speaking full time and never looked back.

The Passion Factor

As a speaker, being passionate about your topic is critical, and it is for your book as well. If you present in a "canned" manner, your audience will know. Your **Passion** is essential to keep your presentations alive and lively—you must care about your topic, your book, your writing. The average book is closed by page 18. Is yours engaging? When it is opened, does your reader fall in? When you have *Passion* for your topic, it radiates everywhere—in your conversations with friends; from the stage as you speak; in media-related interviews.

> *As a speaker, being passionate about your topic is critical.*

My *Passion* was seeded from the embezzlement I experienced—a female partner had withdrawn moneys for drugs from a commercial credit line that I had personally guaranteed. The misuse of the funds only surfaced when all the funds were gone, none paid to the many contractors who had provided building services.

I had been duped. I'm not dumb; how did this happen?

Working with the theme of women sabotaging other women—what the problems are; causations, effects and solutions—I've created a career quest that has lasted four decades. With six books on the topic, identified as a pioneer in this domain, and conducting nine national studies, I'm still as passionate about the topic as I ever was. It ticks me off when people undermine other people, but especially women undermining other women.

For you, the *Passion* factor is as critical as breathing. If you don't have it from the start, your book will never develop the roots it needs to survive and thrive. Finding *Passion* can come from curiosity or an event that triggers a quest, such as what happened to me.

That traumatic life lesson started me on a path that led to multiple books, speaking engagements, consulting contracts, and corporate spokesperson positions over a span of 25 years. I became the "go-to" person if there was toxicity and conflict in the healthcare workplace.

The Commitment Factor

Ahhh ... it's the "rabbit hole" for too many. You can have all the passion and vision, but if you aren't committed, you will fail—PERIOD.

Commitment means time, energy, and money.

How much TIME will you put into supporting your book and speaking career?

Writing a quality book is just one side of the commitment triangle: time, energy, and money. It's what you do with it as it comes out of the gate. Speakers should aggressively pre-market within the year prior to publication, letting their contacts know that "the book is coming" and that special speaking discounts will be tied to the launch.

My entire speaking year was booked ahead with the announcement of a new book, which meant the calendar was full, many thousands of books would be sold and that my brand—Dr. Judith Briles, expert in female-dominated workplaces, conflict resolution and toxic employees—was solid.

This is your work ... work that will lead to building your brand and your speaking career. The reason that I landed a cover story in *People* magazine, an article in the *Wall Street Journal*, appearances on *Oprah* and *CNN*, and more than 1,000 media-related events was that I made the time for it. It was just me … not a publicist … working the phones, making the connections, following up and booking slots. It was just me and the ingredient of time.

> *You, the author and speaker, must carve out time to support this new child of yours. You must allot the time to connect with clients; to connect with the media; to write articles and blogs. And you must allot the time to work the appropriate social media channels.*

If you have a book, how much ENERGY will you put into supporting it? As a speaker, how much energy will you put into supporting your speaking career by marketing to meeting planners and decision makers?

Two critical questions … Lots would be an excellent response. No doubt, your vision and passion will be the driving forces. Plus, the factor of money—you have an investment that you want to see a return on. The return can come quickly, or it can evolve over time.

Days—and evenings—will be long. If there ever was a time to take care of you, this is it. Doing any type of media can have you up in the middle of the night being bubbly, insightful, and enthusiastic—yet your body is saying, "Hey, I want to do nothing ..."

Fueling your energy demands that you be selective with where and what you put it into. Two of my long-time Keepers that I share with all my clients are:

> ### Don't do well what you have no business doing.

> ### If you never say "no," your "yeses" are worthless.

Knowing your audience—what your niche is—will help define where your energy should be directed. If it isn't a fit, don't commit!

How much MONEY will you put into supporting your book?

Stories abound about how an author was down to his last $5 on a credit line before the big sale came in ... but this little book keeps you in the real world. Books take money—the creation will be thousands of dollars.

As The Book Shepherd®, putting together the book budget with a new client is the first thing I do. It is spelled out in every one of my proposals. As the author, you are creating a product that could launch or relaunch an amazing journey that could last decades. As a speaker, shouldn't you be doing the same thing? How much are you willing to invest to get you there?

Be realistic ... my books and speaking engagements have grown and fed a family, built a house, and have been my primary support for 40 years. None of it was done on a penny. No one gave me anything. With the combination of books and speaking gigs, money was always there to add fuel to my expanding company and support my family. Its growth came from having a game plan.

The People Factor

My first book, *The Woman's Guide to Financial Savvy*, was published in 1981 the old-fashioned way—with a New York publishing house courting me and doing it up big. Three printings in three weeks, and national TV appearances including *Good Morning America*. It was exciting and successful. But publicity goes away. I had to keep fueling it. I stayed connected with the phone ... and postcards! Remember, my first book was in the '80s ... email wasn't in play. You, the author and speaker, must allot time to support this new child of yours. You must block out the time to connect with clients; to connect with the media;

to write articles and blogs. And you must block out the time to work the appropriate social media channels.

Fast forward to today. You have so many options to stay in contact. Many are free; some will have a fee. What you do to stay connected will be dependent on what works best for you and for your market.

The Platform ... Putting It All Together

Does it work? Yes. The numbers will always tell the story. Your book identifies you as an expert and begins a public brand around your work. Your speeches around the topic add to your expertise and branding. Consulting or coaching that comes from your speaking adds to the branding bucket. Sponsorships from corporations can surface and add to your branding—making you the go-to person in your field.

Your Book(s), Author Status, and Speaking Engagements are critical components of your brand. Now each one—book, author, speaking—requires its own Platform. Don't think you can become a sought-after speaker without them.

Where a movie set needs lights,
camera, actors and action;
your speaking set needs a website,
clear understanding of who your
audience is, a method to reach out
and market to decision makers
who can hire you ...
and of course, presentations.

3

The Costs of Speaking ...
Create a Spending Plan
for Your Success

*When I'm focused, I finish; when I'm not,
I don't. I bet you are the same way.*

Starting down the speaking path takes planning
and it's not a freebie journey. You will be
"investing" money in a variety of support items.

Depending on what you already have, your "setup" could be a few hundred or many thousands of dollars. Some are obvious:

- Website makeover
- Speaker photos
- Video reel
- Media kit
- Customer management software
- Marketing materials
- Coaches

Then there's time. And you will be investing your energy. Building a speaking career doesn't happen overnight.

> *Most times, newbie speakers*
> *are clueless on where to begin.*

For a visual map of things you need, I created the *Speaking GamePlan Model*™.

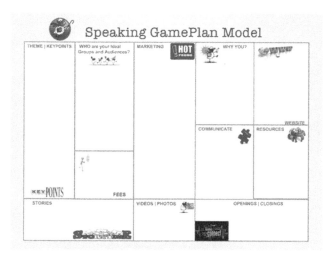

Creating Your Speaking GamePlan

I'm visual and like to have "it" all in front of me when I'm working on a project, which includes anything with my books—whatever "it" is. In creating *GamePlans for Book Marketing, Writing the Book, CrowdFunding,* and now *Speaking,* I've found that it helps me get focused and stay focused. When I'm focused, I finish; when I'm not ... I don't. I bet you are the same way.

The *Speaking GamePlan Model* that I created will kick-start the organization needed for your speaking success; it reminds me what is needed to seed and roll out a career in speaking; and I go back to it when I create a new speech.

In my two-day spring and fall event, *Judith Briles Speaking Unplugged*, participants actually get giant copies to work on during the workshop that are taped on the walls of the hotel meeting room so when an idea hits, participants can move to the walls and post on them. When the event is over, they roll them up and take them home—ready to post on their chosen space to visually remind them "DO THIS" versus the typical notes getting buried in a notebook or file ... never to be seen again.

I use a variety of colored sticky notes, different colored pens and markers ... I even draw or glue images to goose me toward the end. Sometimes I add a favorite quote, even a reminder to not do something. I might add a visual "reward" just for me when I reach my goal.

The Speaking GamePlan Model components include:

Why *You?*
You are the star here ... what's so hot about you?
Is it your expertise, your passions, your commitment, your vision, your solutions, your insights, your what? People want to know.

Who is your *Audience?*
It could be broad or narrow. It could be a dominate gender. It could be old or young or a combo. It could be industry specific. It could be groups within an industry. Take time and determine where your best fit is and who really needs your message.

What is your *Theme* and what are your *Key Points?*
These are essential areas to grasp and work on. Both are elementary to the structure of any presentation. And as you evolve in speaking, these can change.

Do you have a *Video* and *Photos*?
Lights, camera, action … a critical component to every speaker is a short video (less than 10 minutes)—the shorter, the better. Known as a reel by many, it is usually composed of multiple clippings of you in action. I'm also a strong believer in having a full presentation, unedited, of you in action. Ideally, you can show a serious side and a fun side in a video. Your goal is to have a compelling clip. One of the ahas is that videos are used to eliminate speakers. You are judged on delivery, content, even what you wear.

Current photos are needed—both black-and-white and color. This is the time to invest a few hundred dollars for a photographer who "gets" speaking and the types of photos you will need. Do you need photos or special images created? Who will do it?

What about *Fees*?
Have you thought about what you will charge? Will there be a range for keynotes (60-90 min.)

and half-day/full-day workshops? How will you negotiate with limited budgets of groups? Will you speak for free? When will you start charging?

How and when will you *Communicate*?
Do you have a newsletter or ezine? How often do you blog? What about using reminders such as postcards? Do you know where your customers hang out on social media (meeting planners, conference coordinators, program directors, individuals in your target speaking market who fill your audiences)? All are part of your potential team. Granted, some may not know it yet.

***Stories* are crucial for speaking success.**
What are yours? How can you use them as a tool to relate your message?

***Openings* and *Closings* are the bookends to your talk.**
What is compelling? What pulls in the audience? What leaves them with a take-action frame of

mind? Which bookend will will make them feel they are in the right place?

Where are you on *Social Media* and the *Internet*?

Social media and search engine optimization (SEO) are essential to your success. Use key words and phrases as you blast out to the cyber world in posts and images of your expertise and speaking power. You want to be found, pronto. You need a following—lots and lots of followers, friends, and fans. Start building.

Who are your *Resources*?

Who do you need on your team to pull this off? Virtual assistants; friends with plenty of social media contacts; a speaking coach to make sure your presentation content is crisp and has a strong call to action, and is compelling with timing woven in. Who?

What will your *Marketing* efforts consist of?

If you think your phone will ring off the hook automatically or that your emails will load up, think again. Marketing takes time; it needs a plan. And it needs persistence. Who and where you want to speak begins your marketing efforts. What will you create to support your marketing with material about you? Is it a brochure? A media kit? Is it a postcard campaign? Is it doing freebies to start building buzz? What?

What to *Charge*?

It's always a question I'm asked—and an important one. Most times, newbie speakers are clueless on where to begin. Often, they feel that their worth is basically worthless because of their lack of experience. It's this lack of confidence in what they can do on the stage that creates the quandary.

My response: Didn't you write a book on this topic? Or, didn't you just complete your doctorate? Or, didn't you power through and overcome a traumatic experience/adversity? All of that has a value to it.

> *Please, put a value
> on what you bring.*

Where you speak will be a factor.
Let Google help out. Search competitive
speakers—other experts in your field: *speaking
fees for* _____. What comes up? Don't expect to
get top dollar ... but set a minimum fee. I wouldn't
go out for less than $500 ... then move it up
quickly as the word gets out. Some groups don't
pay (think your local Rotary as an example ...
but state and national Rotary functions often
do). If you have a book, you can "make a special
offer" to get around it: *In celebration of my new
book, I'm waving my speaking fee for the first
10 groups who invite me to present.*

What you are doing is getting your foot in the
door. You want to start moving your fees up—
$1,000 usually means you are a beginner;
$2,500 more experienced, etc. Many meeting

planners don't think you are worth much unless there is at least a $3,500 to $5,000 price tag on your services. It doesn't mean that you can't negotiate to work within their budgets. But please, put a value on what you bring.

My goal is to get speakers moving from free to fee as soon as possible. The best of the best of speakers do freebies. For me, I do about 10 a year. When I decide who I do them for, I look at it in two ways:

1. I feel passionate about the group. I want to give to them.

2. I believe that there are members in the audience who can hire me at my full fee.

Otherwise, I say no and refer them to another speaker. As a newbie, gladly accept unpaid speaking gigs that desire a speaker in your topic area. Why? It is an opportunity to tweak content and fine-tune your presentation style. An ancient cliché but ... hey ... practice makes perfect.

4

Starting the Buzz Factor ...

Creating a buzz is essential in building your reputation and filling your speaking calendar.

It all starts with knowing who your market is and focusing on where they hang out. Your goal is to be seen ... and heard.

What professional magazines and journals does your market read? What associations would your market be members of? What types of media might have an interest in your topic and expertise? What book awards would garner merit?

When it comes to creating a press or media release, there is always an "About Me" short bio at the end. It's a boilerplate format, but make sure it has your name (correctly); expert in (or author of); your website and email. Word limit may be in play. Sometimes you can include a fun line or call to action: Get her free copy of ___ (think of your Opt-In or a special offer via your website).

To kick-start your buzz, below are 10 ideas:

1. *Follow bloggers who are "like-minded" and known in your area of expertise.* Make comments and add to others. The goal here is to get your name recognized so others will cross over and discover you.

2. *Add to your own blog on a consistent basis.* Ideally, twice a week. Then post out to your other social media platforms that you have a new blog—the topic/tease to attract them to your site.

3. *Make sure you create an Opt-In piece on your own website.* It could be a Tips Sheet

around your expertise; something fun; something meaty; but something that would attract a meeting planner or a follower of your expertise.

4. *Discover* HARO-Help a Reporter Out, *HelpAReporterOut.com* and Pitch Rate, *PitchRate.com.* Add you name as an "expert" to PitchRate and keep an eye on your category with the HARO emails that are pushed out a few times a day.

5. *When you get media inquiries, respond to them quickly—not next week.* Most reporters are on a tight deadline.

6. *Book award time pops up in the spring and usually end of year.* Saying you are an award-winning author carries clout.

7. *In your niche, identify trade journals and/or association magazines that you can offer an article to.* This is an excellent gateway to speaking at state and national conferences.

8. *Create a newsletter or an ezine that goes out at least once a week.* Make sure that you create it in a mobile-friendly format.

9. *Identify the top media outlets—print, radio, TV, podcasts, and bloggers.* Within the print, radio, and TV formats, are there programs or reporters who write about and around your expertise? Read them. Make comments via social media and letters to the editors. Even call if appropriate and give them a pat on the back. Drop them a note—send a postcard. Visibility is the game here.

10. *Outside of a book, what else have you created?* Is there a special webinar? What about an online course? Then, reach out to those you know—offer a type of joint venture. They should shout out to their followers; host a webinar or teleseminar featuring you. If anything is sold, you split the proceeds.

What happens is your name is out there and you never know who is listening or watching. Maybe a meeting planner. And maybe, someone who belongs to a group who is looking for a speaker with your expertise!

Creating a buzz is essential in building your reputation and filling your speaking calendar. My call to action to you is to make "being seen and being heard" a priority. It supports your expertise and creates, then maintains, the momentum you want as a sought-after speaker.

For a speaker,
you don't need
an MBA or a PhD ...
what you need is
a degree in being GOOD.

5

The Power of the Niche Speaker

As a niche speaker, you know your field inside and out. You are an expert.

Judith Briles, ©TheBookShepherd.com

Highly successful speakers know what their niche is and where their niche can be found. If there is ever a formula for failure, it's the one where the speaker believes, truly believes, that his or her topic or expertise is suited for every audience.

The truth is: the more you niche yourself and your work; the more you "drill down" into that niche; the greater the success you have in your marketing and in the reception of your presentation. And you will sell more books if you have them when you speak. And sell your books at a discount as a perk to the organization that engaged you.

Some speakers "know" their market instantly. Many struggle to find it. Some "think" they know their market, only to discover that another one is a far better fit.

Count me in here. I've have three distinct niches. The first was in the personal finance area and with the drill-down—women and money. The second was in organization behavior and with the drill-down—toxic female dominated workplaces, specifically in health care and nursing. And now my third niche is book publishing and

with the drill-down directed toward the
self- and independent-publishing avenues.

> *If you want to turn
> your niche into a cash cow,
> you've got to figure out what
> the "pain" is that your
> niche is experiencing.*

You can become an expert in an industry without
initially working in it. You do this by reading; by
interviewing other experts within the industry;
by subscribing to journals and magazines that
are exclusive to it; and by attending conferences
as a participant. Sometimes you go to niches; and
sometimes, they come to you. Opportunities are
everywhere. Be open to them and embrace those
that feel right.

As a book and speaking coach, I cannot emphasize
enough how crucial it is to hook your name and
brand to a niche market.

- You—and any talk you create—is not for everyone. The more you narrow your market, the more likely you will find success.

- When you target your niche market, it enables you to craft keynote speeches and workshops, allowing you to hit the nail on the head.

- As you drill down, you will learn more about an industry or environment. Seek out the problems being faced and with your expertise, then deliver solutions woven with stories that are exclusive to that specific industry/environment.

- You become one of "them"—the "go-to" speaker, trainer, person to enlighten and solve problems.

Genders, generations, cultures, and organizations look at situations from different perspectives. They seek solutions and receive information in different ways. What is seen as humorous, dramatic, or thrilling varies widely. And, definitely remember, what is important or crucial to one organization's growth and success likely is unique to that organization.

Building yours ...

If you want to turn your niche into a cash cow, you've got to figure out what the "pain" is that your niche is experiencing. Your niche will turn into fans—fans that will tell their colleagues that "you are the one" and they will do a happy dance around the meeting planner who brings you in.

As a niche speaker, you know your field inside and out. You are an expert. You have special knowledge and keep up-to-date with changes and trends. You don't have to worry or study industries that are unconnected—they are not your niche. When you present, you are weaving your stories with experiences, expertise, and solutions.

The single best way to claim a niche is to publish. When I published my first book about women undermining other women, it was general. When I refocused and wrote about women working in health care, my expertise and reputation grew in that niche. I became the go-to person to speak at nursing conferences on the topic.

Know your "tribe": The one that desperately needs your message; the one that you have studied and know inside and out; the one that you put your time and energy into. No, you don't speak for the masses.

You need to know and then find your tribe.
When it comes to your success as a speaker,
it is so much easier being the whale in the pond
vs. the sardine in the sea.

My call to action for you is to find your special
audience and be a niche speaker.

Branding is recognition
that is built-it's the relationship
between you and your customer.
You carry it throughout your website,
your books, your blogs, you ...
wherever you are. When others see it
or hear, they connect with you.

6

Sparkle with Your Branding

*Your branding should be easy, memorable,
and less than seven words.*

Begin with your **Speaker Branding**. It starts
with focus: What do you do? What do you offer?
You may be a character speaker—someone
who "dresses" the part and wherever you are
speaking, you're instantly recognized. You may
be a business speaker, so showing up in a gypsy
outfit would not be a fit.

*As a speaker,
clarity on what you do is
essential to convey to meeting
planners and to your audience.*

Defining and demonstrating a clear and succinct mission statement should be created along with a personal tagline that others hook immediately with who and what you are and do—as The Book Shepherd, not only have I trademarked the phrase, I've woven in two taglines:

>*Creating successful authors with practical publishing guidance.*
>(my mission)

>*Creating books that clients never regret.*
>(my goal)

When you take a tour of many of the top marketing taglines of well-known companies ... they are less than SEVEN WORDS. Memorable. Easy. Solid.

Years ago, when my daughter was expecting her second child, she wanted a new car that would handle her growing family. But most importantly, at the top of her list was safety. The #1 car that consistently surfaced was Volvo. And guess what its brand was?

Safety ... it had locked in the word. When Volvo first introduced the All-American family car in its line— "safety" soared its first-year sales above all competitors. My Sheryl was a buyer along with millions of others. Safety was what was essential for her family.

As a speaker, clarity on what you do is essential to convey to meeting planners and to your audience who read the description in the program. Your brand is what is in the "head" and "heart" of your buyer—that meeting planner and audience participant. It needs to be woven throughout your website and all your content. It's what you use in your social media outreaches. It's integrated into your essence as you share stories and offer solutions when you are on stage.

Finally, what is distinctive about you? What sets you apart from thousands of other speakers? It's shout-out time. You do it with your colors, your website, your business card, and your clothing. Wherever you are—in person, online, or in media formats—what do you want to convey?

1. Speakers need to find their mojo.

Usually, it's seeded with branding. The key question that you need to answer right now is: *What do you stand for?*

- YOU, the Speaker
- Social Media
- Branding and Message
- Building a Dedicated and Responsive Following
- Product Development (that's your Speech menu plus Books or other items you offer)
- Website Do's and Don'ts
- Content and Blogging

If your immediate response is there is sooooo much I stand for, stop now. Whittle that response down. Narrow it. Get concise. Say it out loud.

Now, in just a few words ... *What do you stand for?*

For me, when I have on my Book Shepherd hat, it's *book publishing excellence*. In two words: *author success*. In my previous career that spanned 20 years in the healthcare workplace, it was *zapping conflict* and *dealing with toxic coworkers*. When I was a stockbroker, it was *women's financial success* and *financial savvy for women* that were the key words. But for my audiences, each connected. Although, I will confess that in health care, a longer phrase was loved: *How to deal with pit bulls with lipstick.* That was a runaway winner.

If you can't get it down to just a few words, how do you expect your customers, your audience, to identify you? To tag you? To remember you? In branding, you need to know what exactly you bring to the customer party.

- **What are your skills, your attributes, even your personality?**
  This becomes the foundation that you build upon.

- ***What sets you apart from others who do what you do?***
  What makes you unique? What sets you apart from the pack?

- ***What will you deliver to your audience or customer?***
  Will you share actionable steps that could assist in solving a troubling problem? Will you unscramble a laundry list of things that there is confusion about? Do you have a healing message? What do you want the takeaway benefits to be?

- ***What feelings will you leave your audience with?***
  Feelings are powerful and this is where pure magic can happen. Will they be elated? Mesmerized by the OMG experience that you just delivered? Tickled pink with the aha that dropped in? Will they feel more confident in handling a sticky situation? Be aware of the feelings that your message can evoke!

2. A *Website* checklist—items that aren't normally asked or included are critical to probe. Anyone who thinks that websites are minor players are ignorant in today's online world. The website is now the hub of everything you do online—from capturing leads, to connecting with others, to selling your speaking services and other products. It's the essential business card. Start with: Do you have a specific tab that says "Speaking" on it? Does it have drop-downs with items such as Introductions; Photos; How to Work with You; Room Setups; or your Calendar that will show availability?

3. What you put on your website is *Content*—make sure it's the right content to match your message and your brand. How do you develop content to keep your website, once up, from being stagnant? Make sure you add your live Facebook or Twitter feed—it keeps the search engine optimization (SEO) happy.

> *Once you truly know what you stand for,*
> *can say it clearly and succinctly,*
> *the business of speaking becomes*
> *so much easier.*

4. What about *Blogs*—do you provide meaty content that supports your expertise as well and provides info for your fans? And what about something for meeting planners, as in a *Tip Sheet to Setting Up a Room; Essential Tips on Hiring a Speaker; 3 Secrets to Maximize a Speaker with Any Group.*

A must on your website is a Speaking TAB that contains information about your presentations and you. They could include:

- Title, short description, and bulleted takeaways for the audience
- Images of you speaking—both still shots and video

- Short Video—sometimes called a reel or demo (anything from short clips of you speaking to a full presentation)
- Speaker One-Sheet
- Kudos from past attendees is HUGE but include meeting planner comments, too

In addition, a subsection could be designated for meeting planners. This could include:

- Introduction to be used by meeting planners at gigs
- Room setup preferences
- Pre-program questionnaire
- Requirements related to travel
- References with contact name, group, phone, and email

5. Your website *List Building* is critical. That means your website needs to be a "collector" of emails from the get-go. You want to create a free "opt-in" piece that serves as a magnet to those who land on your site. Opt-in pieces can range from eBooks to tip sheets around your expertise and everything in between. To get them, an email needs to be given (and usually a name as well). Once done, the item is emailed to the individual and your email manager adds the new email to your growing list.

6. If you have other *Products* (remember, as a speaker, you are a product), your website can have a Product or Store tab. You can add eBooks, DVDs, online courses, coaching, special events or conferences, even a membership circle.

7. *Social Media*, and the top networks of Facebook, YouTube, Twitter, LinkedIn, Google+, Pinterest, and Instagram, as well as any platforms that are appropriate for your audiences, need to be identified. Remember, in using social media you want to provide content, not direct pitches—at least, in most cases.

Providing content builds trust ... and a type of engagement with you and your followers and followers-to-be. When you do have an announcement, they are forgiving. Create posts that might have a countdown to it (only two days left; last day to enroll, etc.).

After an event, do a shout-out to a client or conference name. Include a few images. Make sure you use @CompanyName if on Twitter, or if they are live on Facebook or one of the other social media formats, the appropriate name to link to. Ask the meeting planner if it would be appropriate and clarify what link to use. If you get the green light, you will earn points here. When posting, keep this in mind:

- Is your post word-of-mouth worthy?
- Is your post inspiring?
- Does your post have a call to action?
- Is your post interactive?
- Are you incorporating hashtags within your posts?

8. *Calls to Action* are critical. Refer often to these numbered elements. You need all of them. They are the sparks to keep your author status and book/s plugged in. Don't use social media in a lame manner. It's an amazing and massive tool that has a variety of options to support you and your speaking. Start with the main social media platforms that are relevant to your genre and expertise and deep-dive into the ones that work well for you.

If necessary, get a website makeover. Always be thinking "what else." What other products can you develop using your expertise and book as the foundation? Work on building your crowd; fans are important. And keep building on your content.

- Meeting planners use social media. When they know your name and when they are looking for an "expert in _____," are you findable online? Does your name or something you are connected with surface on the first page of a Google search?

- Reporters and producers use social media. When they know your name and when they are looking for an "expert in _____," are you findable online? Does your name or something you are connected with surface on the first page of a Google search?

- Key individuals in corporations, associations, and groups use social media. When they know your name and when they are looking for an "expert in _____," are you findable online? Does your name or something you are connected with surface on the first page of a Google search?

Is Dress Part of Branding?

It can be. Years ago, the dress for success guy, John Malloy, convinced many that there was a corporate uniform to embrace for all: a suit for both men and women. Really? That was a gagger for me. My body didn't take well to suits. I quickly adapted to black pants or a long skirt; a shell or turtleneck and a colorful silk over-blouse or lightweight long jacket; and low-heeled shoes. My feet and ankles didn't take well to heels, either. Plums and purples were my

Dressing for the Platform

thing and part of my branding colors. Jewelry was restricted to a watch, earrings, maybe a necklace and a bracelet. I was comfortable and could move about easily. Packing was a cinch for the road. I went with colors that I looked good in and felt good in. Suits weren't me.

My suggestion is to ALWAYS dress at least one grade above what your audience is wearing. Ask your meeting planner how attendees will be dressed. I knew that when my gig was at a resort, the apparel would be casual.

Have your colors done. Learn how to wear the ones that complement you, not overpower you or make you look sickly.

Men still use the traditional suit and can perk it up or down, depending on the group and event. Ties add the color. When casual, sports coats are common.

And please, "dress your age" … meaning that those cute and trendy styles for a 20 year old are most likely a total mismatch for a 45 year old. Use your common sense.

Whew! It's time for you to check out your website and everything that you produce using their eyes—how you present yourself; what content you deliver; are you reachable; and is your website presented with an ease of navigation. What separates you from the pack of other speakers and experts in your field; what do you do better than anyone else; and do you connect with their heads and hearts? Once you truly know what you stand for, can say it clearly and succinctly, the business of speaking becomes so much easier.

Part 2:
Must-Have Tools

**If you want to speak ...
you need a website.
No exceptions.**

7

Your Website Needs to Snap, Crackle and POP!

Your website is all about getting noticed. It's about being a magnet to support your speaking success.

Is your website noticeable? Does it clearly say who you are? Does it reveal what you want a meeting planner to know about you? All this and more needs to be on your website. Of course, you will have an ABOUT YOU tab. BLOG tab … but what else? If you are doing any media, add a MEDIA tab. Press releases will go in here. If you have books or other products, a STORE tab. If you have a NEWSLETTER or EZINE, add a tab as well. You need a SPEAKER tab for sure. Within the SPEAKER tab will be a variety of items that are created for the meeting planner.

- Is your name immediately visible when the site opens?
- Is the website easy to navigate?
- Do you have contact info that is easily accessible that includes email, phone number, and street address?
- Can a planner know quickly what you offer?
- Can a planner determine if you do keynotes, workshops, trainings, or webinars?
- Do you have a bio that is compelling?
- Do you have a One-Sheet?
- Do you have different length bios?
- Do you have introductions that can be used at a gig?
- Are there testimonials that show you rock?
- Do you have a variety of photos that could be used in conference brochures in high resolution (color and black-and-white)?
- Do you have your book cover image in high resolution?
- Are there references that are reachable?

- Are there titles and descriptions of presentations that you offer?
- Are there images of you in action?
- Is there a video clip (a reel) of you— either a short (less than 5 minutes) or a full-length one?
- Do you have a blog that has, at the minimum, weekly updates?
- Do you have an Opt-In piece that is designed to be a "magnet" to gather names and emails of visitors?
- Do you have a calendar posted that shows dates you are already booked—including the locations?
- Is there anything on your website that is irrelevant or distracting to a "buyer" of your speaking services?

Your website is all about getting noticed. It's about being a magnet to support your speaking success. It's essential for you not to be wishy-washy. When I had a meeting planner on the phone, I would routinely ask, "Is your computer online?" If he or she responded that it was, I would suggest going to my website right then so I could walk him/her through it. Only taking a few minutes of his/her time, I was now on the radar and follow-up would be easier. After this phone call, I would immediately send out a post-card with my book cover on it and a short note of thanks and that I looked forward to the opportunity of working with him/her.

It's opportunity knocking. Are you ready?

Getting Noticed Takes Planning

Let me ask again, *What do you stand for?* It's essential to be clear on this key question as you develop your speaking website. Speaking is about getting noticed.

When your website is opened ...

1. **At the top of your site in the banner area should be your name—BIG and BOLD.** Your branding starts here. You want a compelling tagline under your name. If you already have a "hot topic" that audiences love ... pull something from that and let it sizzle for you. Here's one I used when I marketed to healthcare groups:

    Dr. Judith Briles ...
    Transforming healthcare workplaces so productivity and retention soar.

2. **Consider showing the result of what you deliver for a client.** When I had an exclusive website dedicated to the healthcare industry ... mine read under my name that was big and bold ...

    When You Zap Conflict in Your Workplace, You Save Millions of Dollars.
    Dr. Judith Briles Will Show You How.

3. **Include a Call to Action.** Meaning, you would like the planner to call or email you.

   To hire YOUR NAME to speak at your next event or purchase her book, BOOK TITLE, connect with her at _____.

When the Phone Rings ... Is Your Checklist Ready?

It's opportunity knocking. Are you ready? Your website isn't a format to apologize for. You want it to say what's needed to be said and to have all the bells and whistles that best communicate your skills. You want it to have items that someone who would hire you would need. A meeting planner should be able to access the following quickly:

- Two-sentence introduction that says who you are and what benefit you bring to an audience.
- Bios—short (50 words), medium (100 words), and long (up to 300 words)

- Introductions—if you speak in a variety of industries, fine-tune them (I had a corporate, dental, nursing, and executive team introduction). Now, I have them for publishing and writing conferences.
- Key takeaways (benefits) that your audience will receive.
- High-resolution images of you as well as your book cover.
- A Call to Action and how to reach you via email and phone.

Above are the checklist items your competitors will have ... and so should you!

A website is a must-have for any speaker.
It's your internet business card with detailed
content on who you are and what you can
deliver to an audience. You may currently have a
website—but how current is it? When was the
last time you had a "makeover"? Do you add
new content on a weekly basis? Does it have
a Speaking tab? And, is it mobile friendly?

8

Have You Created Your Speaker One-Sheet?

A One-Sheet is a snapshot of you—what you do and who you are.

"A one-sheet?" you ask. Yup, a one-sheet, which means it's a sell sheet for you as a speaker. One-sheets can also be for your book, you as the author, your expertise ... and some are a combo. I'm talking about creating a slick one-sheet that brags about you—in the case of a speaker, it needs to be a combo—your expertise and your speaking.

Sometimes it's referred to as a pitch-sheet. Think of it as a snapshot of you—what you do and who you are. You don't want it complicated. It should be simple to read, visually attractive with a little eye candy (images, callouts, sidebars, bubbles, colors), with brag information focusing on you, and your expertise as the best of the best, including your book, if you have one!

Putting together a one-sheet is similar to a puzzle. Don't expect to finish it in an hour. It will contain:

- Expertise claims
- Images
- Your picture
- Contact info
- Connecting info
- Bragging rights
- Numbers
- Writing for the "buyer"
- Testimonials
- Attractive graphics
- Ease of reading

Start with a Combination Statement

In your first sentence, state your expertise/ talents and your bragging rights. Start with power and pop.

What are your shout-outs? Your achievements? Have you got some numbers to back you up that you can reveal? They could be book sales, speaking gigs, awards, media coverage, books printed, rights sold ... what else?

Who's Your Buyer?

It's not everyone. Who wants your services? Your expertise? What will entice them?

My One-Sheet Quest

One of my personal goals for 2017 was to create a spanking new one-sheet that included my expertise. I intended to use it as a door opener for speaking at writers' and publishing conferences as well as connecting me with potential book publishing consulting clients. I needed to demonstrate that I "got" what publishing was; that I had walked the talk multiple times; that I had successfully published with traditional publishers as well as on my own and had sales to support it; and that I had strong testimonials.

I then called Annie Harmon of Harmony Designs in Colorado and one of the graphic artists that I work with who I felt would be the right fit for my new project. After telling her what I was up to, getting an estimated price, I promised to have the content for her to work on within 24 hours. What I did have to immediately forward was easy and accessible on my computer: my name, tagline, several photos of myself, and some of the book awards I'd won.

By the end of the day, I forwarded my opening paragraph—and my only paragraph—to her that was a combo "brag" with achievements that would fit publishing, reinforce expertise, multiple testimonials, contact info, specific programs I do, and a variety of speaking topics. By the next morning, a rough draft arrived of Annie's proposed layout with my colors, fun bubbles for testimonials, and sidebars for contact information. She had selected one of the photos, and decided to display book spines. I wasn't sure if her intent was to feature my published books or my clients' books. I decided my clients' books would be best, but I would horizontally pile the five that I authored on publishing topics and ignore my 30 other books. The "raw" book section looked like this:

"SOS" emails went out to two of the book designers that I work closely with. Sharing what I was up to, I asked if they could forward high resolution book spines of dozens of the authors' books we had created recently. And they came in. Spines were dropped into their places, then adjusted for book heights. Content was modified. My solo paragraph was morphed five times. When I thought I had it all in place, I called bragging expert Jeannette Seibly and read it to her. She insisted I redo the first sentence to nail down numbers to support my own expertise from the get-go. I did what she said. I then sent it to Publicity Hound Joan Stewart for her input. She tweaked a few lines and sent it back. They were both happy, and right.

See my final Ta-Dah on the following page (until I change it again, which the publication of *How to Create a $1,000,000 Speech* will require)!

Most likely, you won't use all of your awesome numbers, all of your achievements, or reveal all of your array of skills and talents. I sure didn't. All the info I had supplied couldn't be used … oh, it could have been if an 8-point font had been engaged—but the "ease of reading" would have disappeared.

If you don't have a one-sheet for yourself, start noodling one. Don't rush it. Engage a graphic designer to add visual pizzazz and when done, save it as a pdf and get it posted on your website.

It's a must-have for every speaker.

9

You Need an Online Media Kit

You want to demonstrate you aren't a newbie.

Yes, oh yes, you do. A Media Kit is important for speakers. Meeting planners check them out. In reality, most "experts" and those who call themselves experts have a media or press kit. Unless your game plan is to remain invisible, you need one. It's expected; it's useful. Get over your reluctance to add one to your website. You've probably heard of HARO: Help a Reporter Out. It's online and you get several emails a day broken into topic areas. Reporters and media are looking for pros and experts in a variety of fields. Guaranteed, yours pops at least weekly. And it's free.

You may be using it now. Or you may not know about it ... but you should. If you are seeking book publicity—yes, any free media exposure— it's a source.

But your website is your #1 resource. On it you need:

- to create a Media or Press tab on the toolbar on the Home page of your website. Your Media/Press tab adds to your online searchability: SEO (very important).

- an author and/or speaker press kit.

- any press releases (make sure they have dates on them).

- your contact info—all of it: phone (land and cell); email and snail mail address; Twitter and Facebook address.

- to make sure you include the right information.

- to deliver it in a format that's easy for all journalists to use (both downloadable pdfs and Word document and jpgs for photos).

- to have high- and low-resolution photos of you and your book cover (jpgs usually preferred).

> *The* **PublicityHound.com** *is rich with information for media resources.*

- to start gathering any interviews that are in print (ask sources for a pdf, otherwise scan).

- to start gathering logos of radio, TV, and print companies that you are quoted or featured in (you will create a snazzy display on your website with these— great for building credibility).

Blunders and Boo-Boos to Avoid

You, me, and everyone else make mistakes. Getting it all right is usually impossible, at least in the first go-around. But, you can do much yourself. Media pros can be very expensive. I'm a firm believer in learning how to pitch yourself and supply the "accents" that will hook the media. And, I don't think you need to hire a PR expert to put it together, and get it done.

Publicity pros like the Publicity Hound Joan Stewart have excellent resources in template format that you can readily use for minimal dollars. Joan's website, *PublicityHound.com*, is rich with information. I highly recommend you get her *Author Media Kit* immediately. It's an easy-peasy, step-by-step how-to in putting together what you need that is media friendly.

The most common mistakes include:

1. Being lost—your media spot/room isn't findable or visible

It doesn't matter what you call it as long as it shouts out "media info here." Common names for the tab might be:

Press, Press Room, Press Kit
Media, Media Room, Media Kit
News, Newsroom
PR, Publicity
Buzz Media
Media
Press

Many have a section on their sites simply identified as "Media" or "Press." If a reporter or producer is on your site and sees any of the above, they will assume it contains a media kit. Unfortunately, most don't. What they usually have is a mishmash of articles or links featuring the website owner, and maybe some photos. Yes, these are recommended for inclusion, but you need more. You want to demonstrate that you aren't a newbie. Make sure that there are articles and links to interviews or shows that you've been on.

I've been on thousands of radio and TV shows over the past 30 years and featured in countless print formats. Here's what we did with just a few of their logos:

Judith in the Media

2. Little or no contact information

If there is a button-pusher for me on a website, this tops the list. Really, what were you thinking when you made it impossible to reach out to you? When it comes to the media, it wants instant connection if you, your topic, your expertise is what they are looking for—and ditto with meeting planners for speaking gigs.

If you have a media page, you want the media to contact you ... yes? Make it easy. Imagine a reporter or a meeting planner doing a Google search for experts in your topic area and your name, an article, blog and/or website appears on Google's first page. Although there are hundreds of pages, maybe thousands, roughly 90 percent of searches stop on page one. Good news for you ... or is it? When the searcher clicks through, he or she is intrigued and wants to immediately call you. The question is: Can it happen? Or, will a "walk-away" happen? You are hidden—a phone number can't be found; an email isn't there.

Maybe it didn't occur to you that someone might want to contact you for an interview; to ask a few questions about your topics and audiences; or to hire you.

Do not, do not, do not send them to your "Contact" to fill out a form with blanks on it. Make it EASY—give them your relevant information up front.

This misstep could cost you a speaking gig—or a publicity opportunity.

3. Images are MIA

When it comes to images, think the more, the merrier. At a minimum, you need a professionally done head shot (several shots are even better). You also need your book cover image.

Make them available in both high-resolution ("high-res" is 300 dpi or greater) and low-resolution ("low-res" is less than 300 dpi). Print publications and TV need high-res images; bloggers and websites are okay with low-res.

Your images should never be missing in action on your website.

Include both black-and-white and color photos. Have a variety. And, don't be afraid of including a casual look.

4. Press materials are only in pdf format

There's an unwritten rule that you don't send anything via email unless it's a pdf. On your website, in your media section, think differently

... or at least, in addition to. Meaning that, yes, create a pdf of the media release, but also create a Word document ... a duplicate. This allows a copy/paste version that any producer/reporter/meeting planner can quickly extract information from and drop it into what they are working on. Trust me, they will thank you.

5. There's no date on your press releases ... add them

Get into the habit of posting an UPDATED press release about you.

Visitors want to know if what you are posting is "dated" or "current." Add the date to all press releases. And, if you are concerned about older releases, why don't you create a new one? Surely you have news that you want to share: information about an event; a speaking gig you are keynoting; or a book award that you have won.

A Media tab is usually ignored on a website. Granted, most likely you won't have a lot in it when it first goes up. But time and effort will change that. So don't ignore your Media tab.

Remember: You can immediately include photos. You can create a page with questions to be used in an interview. And, you can create a press release around your book or book-to-be. It's a beginning.

10

Yes, You Need a "Canned" Introduction

It's not uncommon for the introducer to stumble over the copy and mispronounce the simplest of names, which could be yours.

Part of any speaking gig is to be **introduced.** It's the "setup" to you and your message. Wouldn't you like it to be perfect?

Yes, you would. Yet it often doesn't happen. Having delivered 1,000+ presentations, I've heard my name botched, the title of my presentation misstated or blatantly wrong, and at times, nothing like I emailed or snail-mailed to the meeting planners.

Can you prevent delivery snafus? Not always. Can you reduce the occurrence? Definitely.

- Start with creating your own Introduction.

- If your name is unusual, tell them how to pronounce it in the Intro (my last name—BRILES—rhymes with SMILES).

- Put in pauses using an ellipsis ... creating "punch" for listeners.

- Let the introducer tell them you have books available for sale after your presentation and where you will be signing them—people like signed books! If appropriate, the introducer can let audience know that you are offering books at a discounted price to all attendees. Be generous—think a 10-20 percent discount. You should not be the money collector. My husband traveled with me and handled the store. If you are solo, mingle early and ask if anyone would like to help you at the book table.

Usually, several will be delighted to be your assistant—give them a book or something else as a "thank you."

- Include your picture on it (current one) ... your introducer wants to "see" who you are—he or she may not have met you prior to when you are introduced.

- Create your introduction in a font that is 14- or 16-point, bold, and double-spaced.

- Have it on your website under your Speaker tab.

- Send it to to the meeting planner.

- If the meeting planner isn't introducing you, ask who is—call for a short hello; thank him or her for introducing you; and if you have an unusual name, go over its pronunciation.

- Have a printed copy with you at the event as a backup.

It is not uncommon that the role of introducing you is handed off to someone and not a lot of thought is put into the "who" that someone should be. Sometimes, he or she is nervous; sometimes a poor reader; sometimes a winger; and it's not uncommon for the introducer to stumble over the copy and mispronounce the simplest of names, which could be yours. Sometimes, your carefully penned introduction goes missing.

You want your introducer to be your supporter. If you have a book, be prepared to give away signed copies—to your introducer, host sponsor, helper at the book table, etc. Have a printed intro copy with you—in double-spaced, bold, and at least a 14-point font. If your intro is MIA, whoever is introducing you will be grateful for your copy.

You may want a line that will be a "tell" for you based on the audience reaction—i.e., is there laughter? In the introduction I used for my healthcare association audiences, I always included a line or two that based on the audience response, would direct me to know which "opening story" I would use.

Sometimes, I included a range of groups I had spoken to in my Introduction. The purpose: to let a varied audience know that I could handle and interact with a variety of industries, occupations and ages.

Samples

Introduction for Dr. Judith Briles

Dr. Judith Briles is The Book Shepherd and author advocate who excels at working with authors to create books they never regret.

She is the award-winning and bestselling author of 36 books, including ***How to Avoid 101 Book Publishing Blunders, Bloopers & Boo-Boos*** and ***Author YOU: Creating and Building Your Author and Book Platforms.***

To date, her books have been translated into 16 languages with over 1,000,000 copies sold! Her books, and work, have been featured in over 1,000 radio and television shows including repeat appearances on *CNN, CNBC,* and *Oprah.* Print publications include *Newsweek, People, Time,* the *Wall Street Journal,* and ... the *National Enquirer!*

Today, she will speak on _____ .

Please welcome Judith Briles.

Introduction for Dr. Judith Briles

Our Speaker today is known as a crazy book lady and The Book Shepherd. Judith Briles is the author of 36 books including ***How to Avoid 101 Book Publishing Blunders, Bloopers & Boo-Boos***. She's worked with more than 1,000 authors and has helped create more than 500 best sellers.

Judith Briles has spoken in front of such diverse groups as the Operating Nurses, the 8th Grade Class of Portola (por-tol-la) Valley Elementary School and the Tank Division of the US Army!

She's been featured on every major TV show from *Oprah* to *CNN* to Waterloo's public

TV station and in the *Wall Street Journal, People* magazine and ... the *National Enquirer.*

Her topic today is _____.

Judith will be with us throughout the conference and available to answer your questions at her book table.

Please welcome Dr. Judith Briles ...

Introduction for Dr. Judith Briles

You are going to spend the next hour with someone who is snappy, sassy and very savvy about book publishing and marketing. The Book Shepherd®, Dr. Judith Briles will deliver the juice to spring all authors to action to achieve their publishing goals ... and that means you!

She has guided 1,000 authors to book completion and generated over 500 best sellers. Today, she delivers ten amazing **Ninja Book Marketing Tips to Soar Your Book Sales**. Make sure you register for face-to-face time with her during the conference. Get her books in our bookstore. Please welcome The Book Shepherd, Dr. Judith Briles.

What to do ... punch up your introduction to match your audience. Post them to your Speaking tab on your website. Your presentation starts before you say one word. Write out what you want the audience to hear ...

Plan on having a variety of introductions to "fit" the occasion. You don't want an intro that is lengthy. Remember, if there is a conference brochure, it usually has your bio info in it. Introductions do not need to be boring. And, unless you are speaking to an academic type of group, you can skip all the degrees and where you went to school. If you've recently been honored with a prestigious award, adding a line about that might make sense.

11

What Do Your Photos Say About You?

*Photos can say you are approachable—
something meeting planners and audiences like.*

What photos are you using on your website? How about for your Speaking tab? How about for your Media tab? Are they oldies, but what you consider goodies? Could they be more than five years old?

Your picture says a thousand words:

- what you do;
- who you are;
- what you love to play with or at;
- what your expertise is;
- who your crowd is;
- what else?

Visuals are powerful. You may use them on your book covers, your website and your promo and publicity material. Think bios, Speaker One-Sheets, website, promo materials and social media. All that showcases your genre and personality.

You've invested in your speaking career. Now, invest in a photo shoot of yourself. It might be a solo shot; it might be you surrounded by new fans or a cheering audience; it might contain items that support your branding; it might capture you "out of your regular element" ... but what it will do is give you a variety of

options to have available for media, your
website, and much more.

What You Need to Determine:

What types of speaker pics do you need?
Ideally, you need a professional head shot. With
the mobile devices we all have with the built-in
cameras, getting headshots and candid shots are
simple. I have been on enough cruises that I
have actually cropped some of the pictures
taken and even used those. Good enough ... but
were they? Do they look professional?

Do those photos really highlight the "best" of
what you want to reflect? Maybe ... but most
likely not.

Stop. You are worth more than any selfie shot
will create. Bypass the selfies. Your book and
Speaker One-Sheet should not look like a DIY
project. Your meeting planners and audiences
will know. Book Sales and speaking engagements

will be impacted. Don't be surprised to discover that many may not pick up your book because it looks mediocre; a meeting planner may bypass you because of the same thing: a mediocre Speaker One-Sheet; mediocre photos; mediocre descriptions; mediocre anything. Ugh.

When I did a self-assessment, I knew it was time to step up my game. Yes, I've had professional shots done through the years ... but it had been a long time. Now I needed to make a phone call and set up a time to get multiple shots for a variety of uses.

Show some action and use different locations. You want both inside and outside ... it changes the look and feel. I host the podcast, AuthorU-Your Guide to Book Publishing. One show was dedicated to the topic of author photography and my expert was Ashlee Bratton. She shared,

If you have a business book, you can use a studio shot or a neutral shot. It can be done

with an indoor or outdoor backdrop. Nonfiction can have a background that can tie into your theme. For example, military books could use a tarmac location, an author coud wear a bomber jacket, use a plane or helicopter if appropriate. A cookbook author naturally fits in a kitchen environment. Fiction books open multiple possibilities. Be creative.

How much should you pay and how to negotiate?

Always a good question ... understand that prices will vary from a few hundred to several thousand dollars, depending on who you work with and what packages the photographer has. You want to be sure to get commercial copyright use and digital files—whatever your portrait package is. And, read the contract and understand it before you sign. Ashlee has put together a terrific all-inclusive package for authors for less than $300. Take advantage of it.

Finally, I took my own advice.
Okay, I did it ... meaning that I settled in and did a photo shoot with photographer Ashlee of Ashography (*Ashography.com*), who just happens to be an author as well—*Life Before the Lottery.*

In the back of my mind, I knew ... *yes, I knew,* that I had to step up and get a professional photo shoot done. She had been after me for a few years to do one. Then, she called my bluff a few months later. "I'm doing a baby shoot next weekend in your area and I have a few hours. I'm coming by and we are going to do a shoot next Sunday," her voice said with confidence.

Gulping, I agreed to be ready. Here are a few from my shoot (see opposite page).

I loved working with her. It was fast, super-casual (my style), and painless. I loved the variety and felt she captured me. Changing earrings a few times and my blouse/jacket plus fresh lipstick ... it was a Ta-Dah!

Do yourself, your book, your fans and followers
a favor. Get another photo shoot scheduled ...
but before you do, make sure you listen to the
show I did with Ashlee to give you all the tips

you need to make it the BEST!
http://bit.ly/AuthorPhotos.

And guess what, Ashlee is bugging me again ... time to do an updated shoot. Why not—this is one from the latest shoot.

It's your turn. What's unique or distinguished about what you do or have done? What kind of "props" can you bring to a shoot? When it comes to a speaker, both meeting planners and audiences like the thought that you are "approachable"—something a photo can say. A poorly done photo can also turn people away from you. The savvy speaker makes sure that his or her photo in a brochure can't be mistaken for someone else. Keep your photo current.

All speakers need photos. Stills. Action shots. Having fun. Reflective. Update every few years and allow yourself to go beyond the smartphone shot. Think of your photos as part of your marketing costs. You don't have to spend a fortune. What you want to do is work with a photographer who gets you; who understands that a professional shot is way beyond what you did in a business suit or cap and gown. Your photo should reflect your personality and your openness to share information with anyone who is in your audience.

Never underestimate
the power of snail mail.
Speaking/Expertise designed
postcards require less postage
and the receiver instantly
sees what has been sent
vs. opening an envelope.

12

The Glory of Postcards

*My boss has had your postcard on her desk
for three months.*

In looking back over my multi-decade speaking
career, in order of importance, here's where my
speaking business came from:

- Being an Expert
- Referrals
- Phone Calls
- Postcards
- Snail Mail
- eMail

In Chapter 19, *Marketing Yourself for Booking
Success*, I mention email, snail mail, and phoning,
and what I did and recommend you do. In
Chapter 21, *Don't Be a Swooper ... the Power of*

Hanging Out!, schmoozing and networking are identified as savvy secrets to selling books and getting referrals.

I also shared that I was a huge sender of postcards—sometimes 50 a day.

On the opposite page is a sample of what I send out for writing and publishing conferences. Note that there are endorsements, speaking topics, and a full bio of who I am on the front. By the time this book is published, there will be postcards for my books: *Author YOU: Creating and Building Your Author and Book Platforms, How to Avoid 101 Book Publishing Blunders, Bloopers & Boo-Boos, The CrowdFunding Guide for Authors and Writers, Snappy Sassy Salty-Wise Words for Authors & Writers,* and of course, *How to Create a $1,000,000 Speech.*

Front and back of one of my marketing postcards
to promote my speaking expertise on publishing:

Dr. Judith Briles

Judith Briles, aka *The Book Shepherd*, has shepherded more than 1,000 authors and created 500 best-sellers and award-winning books. She's knowledgeable, entertaining and has personally authored 35 books that have been translated to 16 languages; sold a combined 1,000,000 copies; and generated in excess of $5,000,000 in revenues from combined book sales and speaking fees.

Judith knows publishing inside and out from both the traditional and independent sides. She is an advocate for authors within her blogs, podcasts and speaking engagements. What's her pet peeve? Two words: publishing predators. She hosts the podcast *AuthorU – Your Guide to Book Publishing* that generates over 100,000 downloads a month and is the Founder of AuthorU.org.

Her website is *www.TheBookShepherd*
email: *JudithBriles.com* phone: *303-885-2207*
Judith is *The Book Shepherd.*

Dr. Judith Briles
8122 S Quatar Circle
Aurora, CO 80016

Publishing Expert and Conference Speaker
Snappy ... Sassy ... Fun ... and Hits the Mark for Attendees

Conference Chairs Are Talking ...

"Judith Briles was not only a phenomenal keynote speaker for our organization, but she wowed our members with three presentations. She is a first-class act all around."
Upper Peninsula Publishers and Authors Association

"There was no better person to help us launch the Author Marketing Event then Dr. Judith Briles. She is a wonderful speaker for any event—we will have her back."
Texas Authors, Inc.

"... our attendees loved you ... and we want you back!"
Las Vegas Writers Conference

Topics include ...
Jedi Book Marketing, Crowdfunding, Crafting a Speech that Sells Books, How to Create the 15-second Pitch, Creating the Platform, Publishing Options for Today, Avoid Book Publishing Blunders

303-885-2207 | Judith@Brlles.com | www.TheBookShepherd.com

On the healthcare side that I worked in for 20 years, I rotated postcards for my books *Zapping Conflict in the Health Care Workplace; Stabotage! How to Deal with the Pit Bulls, Skunks, Snakes, Scorpions & Slugs in the Health Care Workplace; The Confidence Factor;* and *Money Smarts for Turbulent Times.*

As an author of multiple books, I had the advantage of mailing out a different postcard each week for a month, then I started over. Each time a postcard cycled, I added a different note on each of the four.

Was my technique effective? Yes, indeed! In one call, the secretary to one of my recipients answered the phone. She said, "My boss has had your postcard on her desk for three months."

Wow, I thought. Then I asked, "Is she available for a few minutes?"

The call was put through … and in ten minutes, the gig was secured.

Postcards worked for me. I was consistent in how I sent them out.

My strategy would be:

1. First, call on the phone. I kept it very short if I got the person live versus voice mail. If I had already met her, I would remind her where it was (at what event) and added that she had wanted me to call her. If she had asked me to hold a date, I would mention it.

    If I hadn't met the person, I would thank her for taking my call and identify who I was and my expertise. *Hello, Susan, this is Dr. Judith Briles …*

I would ask if there was any conflict within her department or hospital. I would ask if increasing productivity and reducing turnover were important. And then I would see where our conversation would go.

2. Offer to send additional information and/or guide her to my website and refer to a particular feature on it that I thought would be of interest.

3. Thank her again; ask when I should follow up and say goodbye.

4. Send a postcard and schedule another call at time recommended.

5. Send an email with a "tidbit" in the message that I thought might be useful— something about the industry; a news item that could have an impact; maybe something that just is pleasant or meaningful. Again, keeping it short.

6. Make the scheduled follow-up call and
    reconnect.

7. Sometimes, the gig is booked. Sometimes,
    I had multiple holds on a date—we always
    let others know if they were a first or
    second hold, etc. If a firm offer came in,
    we let the holds know and whoever
    committed within 24 hours would get
    the date.

Other times, more follow up is needed.

8. Until I got a "yes" or "no," I would then
    repeat.

This worked successfully for me. Call, mail,
email, call …

Because I was on the road so much, I had to
create a method that was efficient and fast.
When in the office, I could find one to two hours
a day. My assistant worked part-time—three
days a week. If I was on the road when the

follow-up had been scheduled, she would make the call.

1. Introducing herself as my marketing assistant, she told her caller I was speaking to an organization or hospital or traveling to such and such city/state and name the gig by title that I would be presenting, noting if it was a keynote or workshop.

2. Ideally, she would take over from that point and attempt to secure the date. If asked to have me personally call back, I did.

3. Once a date was agreed upon, my contract, invoice for 50 percent of the speaking fee (balance due at time of speaking engagement), and other necessary material were created and both emailed and snail mailed.

4. My marketing assistant would follow up
    in a week to make sure everything had
    been received and remind the contact
    that no speaking engagement was
    considered firm until the signed contract
    and fee deposit was received in our office.

What works for you will depend on your
personality and methodology.

My advice: Never underestimate the power
of snail mail.

As an author,
having a book can be
your tipping point
in getting hired
as the speaker for an event.

13

Why a Book Is the Ultimate Door Opener to Successful Speaking

Embrace and shout out what you excel at.

At every gig that I've ever presented at, there has always been someone in the audience who has approached me and said, "I want to be a speaker like you ...."

It's flattering, but speaking is work. Don't be fooled. Those words; the stories; the movements on the stage that a speaker delivers are choreographed to present an entertaining, enlightening, or inspiring presentation which will move those listening to some type of action.

They don't come in a few hours. It takes mega hours of practice and often years before the "art of speaking" becomes like breathing. And even if the same topic has been presented hundreds of times, there still can be stress and a bit of anxiety in the speaker's air as he or she walks onto the stage.

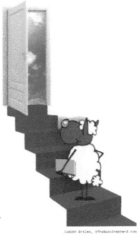

Judith Briles, @TheBookShepherd.com

I was an accidental speaker

My speaking was almost an accident. As a stockbroker in the '70s, I stepped in for another when family obligations prevented her from accepting a speech in the Bay Area of San Francisco to a group of women who were interested in investing. I had never given a formal speech before, but agreed to do it. Looking back, I made so many mistakes that I would caution any newbie speaker from taking on such an obligation. I didn't have a coach to guide me; all I had was knowledge—my years of expertise of doing what I did on a daily basis.

I was one of the very few women stockbrokers at that time and the group wanted a woman to talk to and with them. That I could do. For two hours, I shared a huge amount of information—I had a few notes with me. Mostly, I spoke from a "If you want to be a successful investor ... here are the steps to take" approach.

They loved it. What I didn't know was that casual gathering would seed a new career—one as a speaker and one as an author. From that talk, I developed an all-day class, Women and Money, for a community college. I was amazed—it sold out semester after semester and I got paid for it. From that class, my first (and I thought only) book was written and published, *The Woman's Guide to Financial Savvy*. Little did I know that it would breed many more financial books. From that evening presentation I did for 20 women in the '70s, I eventually became a full-time speaker and author and supported my family for over 40 years.

It all starts with your expertise

I started speaking before I ever thought of writing a book. I was an expert in personal investing. When I started speaking, it hadn't dawned on me that speaking could be a career. Not yet ... that didn't happen until I had book #2 in hand. Then the lights turned on and my plan to stop working for others and start working for myself began to take form.

Speaking is a craft that evolves. Oh, some are natural motor-mouths and outgoing. Don't think their ease means it's no big deal to get up in front of a group.

> *The word "expert" is the most often used adjective in online searches when someone is looking for a speaker on a specific topic.*

If someone comes to me with the "I want to be a speaker" glaze in their eyes, my first responses are:

> Tell me about your expertise ...
> and about you.
> Tell me about your book ...
> do you have one or are you writing one?

And I listen. There's nothing wrong with being a wannabe speaker. Do I sense that this individual really has an expertise ... or did he read a book and now thinks he knows it all? Does this person really have some "in the trenches" experience or do I think she is a faux expert?

> *Books are known*
> *as "lead generators" for speakers.*

The word "expert" is the most often used adjective in online searches when someone is looking for a speaker on a specific topic. As an author, the word "expert" should be used in all your social media profiles, on your website, your speaking introductions ... everywhere.

Books are known as "lead generators" for speakers. With a book in hand, it's easier to get a foot in the door. You are an author. You are published. Corporations like books and the authors that go with them. Associations like authors and routinely offer the author's book for sale at a conference or allow the author to have a table to display and sell books to attendees.

Today, I'm a book and speaking coach and book publishing expert. I definitely have a broad expertise in publishing—in the traditional area, the independent area, and the self-publishing area. As in 35-plus years' worth—I've been published over a dozen times by New York publishers before another light turned on— creating my own publishing company. I've been there, done that ... For me, I can walk and talk and chew gum at the same time when it comes to publishing. I've walked the talk and I can talk the walk.

What paths have you walked? What stories do you have to share that will inspire, motivate, entertain, and change lives? If you don't have a book, it's time to put one in your timeline. Start creating content. Add it to your website. Create blogs. Focus on what you know and tie it into your blogs. Post them. Start a string and before you know it, you will have chapters forming. You have the opportunity to become a thought leader that is findable and shareable.

As a speaker, or a wannabe speaker, it will put you on the fast track in connecting with those that bring in speakers ... and pay them.

I know, I know, I know ... marketing is crucial for your speaking success. Having a book in hand, or one that will be in hand within the year, can be the beginning of a long-running road. And, of course, so are YOU in your development. It's the "expert" in you that came from experience, research ... sometimes just surviving. Embrace and shout out what you excel at—be the go-to brain surgeon, not the guy or gal who can suture a minor cut.

14

WOOT ... You Have a Gig ... Send a Contract!

Your contract is a formal agreement between you and the group that is hiring you.

Speaking Contracts

Judith Briles, TheBookShepherd.com©

It's always sweet music to a speaker's or to the marketing assistant's ears that you are wanted and for a specific date. What do you do next? You send a contract or agreement to engage you. And you do it immediately.

Your contract is a formal agreement between you and the group that is hiring you. It includes speaking fees; what the deposit is and when the balance is to be paid; what you are going to do for them; where the site of the speech will be; who your contact is and contact information; any requirements that you have; a reimbursement clause; and a cancellation clause. In addition to your speaking fee, the client should cover transportation (cabs, Uber, Lyft, etc.), airfare, lodging, meals, and any other miscellaneous expenses you incur on behalf of the engagement.

I'm sharing with you the majority of the elements within my speaking contract. Originally created by my attorney, adjustments have been made over the years. For example, when I had an engagement in one state, my office had booked three speaking events within a few days of each in other states. After leaving my home base, I would be going from airport to airport involving four states. When one had to cancel and change the date, my air ticket created lost time for me and a rebooking of the air ticket—at a cost of over $800 that I had to pay for. A clause was added that stated that if I had to rebook a ticket after being issued and there was an added fee, the changing client would be responsible. Today, most tickets can carry a $200 change fee plus other additional fees. You don't want to be eating these.

Start with:

AGREEMENT TO ENGAGE SPEAKER

We hereby agree to engage YOUR NAME as a speaker for GROUP NAME on DAY/DATE. The presentation will be _____ for a total of ___ minutes/hours.

Your requirements: What type of microphone do you want, whether you need a projector and screen or other items. I always requested a thermos of hot water and cup if I need to wet my throat—especially with workshops.

If you have "educational materials" (such as books) for purchase by participants, include:

> The client will provide a 6-foot table in the main registration open area, main exhibitors' hall or hallway in front of the room in which YOUR NAME is speaking. If there are exhibitors selling books, you may want to include: No exhibitors will sell any of <u>YOUR NAME</u> books or materials during the conference other than <u>YOUR NAME.</u>

Money is important: Note that I have in my clause my regular fee and a final fee. I've done this for when I do "deals" and freebies for some groups. I want them to realize in writing that they are getting something of value. *State what you agreed on:*

> We further agree to pay a net speaking fee of "Final Fee"; this is a reduction of <u>YOUR NAME</u> regular speaking fee of _____ per day. Any taxes or additional fees required by your state or country are the responsibility of your organization.

Now, get a deposit: As in 50% of the agreed fee. It means the group has "skin in the game" ...

otherwise you are going to find yourself chasing money. Also, I let the group know that the speaking engagement wasn't considered "firm" until the deposit and contract were returned to our offices. And, if you aren't paid the balance at the time of the event per your contract, add a penalty. Why? My decades of speaking have shown that the times that I didn't get paid the balance, it was an average of 45 days before I got it. Again why? Simply because the gig is over; other things are now on the group's or the planner's plate. It's not that I (or you) didn't deliver … it's just once you are out of sight, you become out of mind.

An advance retainer in the amount of Deposit Amount is required upon signature of this contract. **Engagement is not considered confirmed until retainer fee and signed contract are received in our office by** Deposit Due Date. Once the date of the program is agreed upon and reserved, the retainer fee is nonrefundable."

"If the retainer is not received in our offices by the due date, the date will be released to other potential clients. The balance of the fee and travel expenses identified in the second invoice should be presented to YOUR NAME at the conclusion of the event. All checks should be made payable to: WHO? Tax ID #_____. A W9 form is attached for your accounting department.

If fees and travel expenses are not paid on the aforementioned dates, finance charges are as follows: a $300 late charge will be assessed with an additional $100 on the fourth day and each subsequent fourth day after your event. Should it become necessary to hire an attorney for the collection of delinquent fees, client is responsible for payments of all attorney, collection fees, and carrying charges.

Handouts: Most likely you will have them. Even when you aren't sharing some of your slides with attendees, I would create a one-page handout with your name, logo, book cover, and key points. Don't forget to include your website, email, and phone number.

Master copy of handouts or workbook will be provided by YOUR NAME for duplication for all attendees in advance of the presentation. Workbook/Handouts are protected by copyright and may only be used in YOUR NAME session. Further duplication requires written permission.

Client's responsibilities: Client will have responsibilities, including your travel, if any; overnight accommodations, if any. If you have a preferred airline, identify it. And, it's wise not to allow your client to give you a ticket it has obtained with frequent flyer miles. If there is a mechanical problem or your flight is cancelled, you may be out of luck in getting rebooked. List what you need.

Client is responsible for the following listed expenses, including any overnight or second day delivery service expenses. Any additional expenses will be billed after the presentation.

Client is responsible for one economy coach airfare from <u>YOUR AIRPORT</u>. When air travel is booked at discounted fares, either separately or as a combination fare with another client, **client is responsible for paying any additional costs once tickets are purchased should the presentation date change or be canceled by client. Our office will book all travel,** including airfare and car rental, at the lowest coach/economy rates available at the time of booking said reservations. <u>YOUR NAME</u> will book coach airfare on PREFERRED AIRLINE.

Closest major airport: _____

Closest regional airport: _____

Hotel ... you want to stay in the hotel of your choice, BUT if the conference is at another, stay there. You need to be onsite with an elevator away from your speaking room. You may wonder about my stipulation below about not being above the 8th floor—it's because fire truck ladders only reach the 8th floor!

Hotel Information:
Hotel accommodations, **Two Nights if necessary**, for YOUR NAME shall be made by client and paid by client. Accommodations must be at the conference site or at a **major full service hotel**, and the room **MUST BE NONSMOKING** with nothing higher than the 8th floor and preferably a king or queen-size bed. Hotel, food, and gratuities are to be billed to client's master account.

Reservations have been made for YOUR NAME as follows:

Hotel Name: _____

Hotel Address: _____

City: _____ State: _____ Zip: _____

Phone: _____ Fax: _____

Date(s): _____

Confirmation #: _____

Client Contact: Upon arrival, YOUR NAME should contact the following person(s):

Name(s): _____

Required numbers for emergencies:

Work: _____ Cell: _____

Venue Information: (If not the same as above)

Site Address: _____

City: _____ State: _____ Zip: _____

Phone: _____ Fax: _____

Date of Presentation(s): _____

Time of Presentation(s): _____

Title of Presentation(s): _____

Due to <u>YOUR NAME'</u>s heavy speaking schedule, a cancellation, other than by an Act of God, causes a loss of income. Therefore, <u>YOUR NAME</u> has found it necessary to include the following cancellation clause:

**100% of fee and any expenses incurred if canceled
Less than 125 days prior to presentation date**

Verification of cancellation shall be given by telephone, followed by a letter to <u>YOUR NAME</u> within five (5) days thereafter.

If <u>YOUR NAME</u> is unable to get to the presentation due to an act of God, including weather, transportation cancellations, breakdowns, or hospitalization, she will credit the deposit paid for a future engagement to be booked and completed within two (2) years of the canceled date. The client and <u>YOUR NAME</u> will mutually determine if she or the client will get a substitute speaker.

Audio and/or video recording of this presentation permitted by prior arrangement only.

<u>YOUR NAME</u> agrees to abide by the professionalism and ethics guidelines set forth by the NATIONAL SPEAKERS ASSOCIATION at all times.

YOUR NAME signed _____

or if you have a Marketing Director, his/her name

AGREED: _____
(Signature of Client)   (Date)

_____
(Name - printed)   (Title)

**DATE WILL BE RELEASED UNLESS ONE COPY OF
THIS AGREEMENT AND THE RETAINER CHECK OF
Deposit Amount ARE RETURNED BY Deposit Due Date
of _____ .**

All correspondence, payments, Federal Express, UPS,
USPS deliveries should be sent to:

**YOUR NAME
ADDRESS**

There you have it ... from me to you. Get what you agreed upon in writing—ALWAYS and with NO EXCEPTIONS. Remember, even when I did freebies and reductions from my regular fee, I used my contract.

15

Pre-Program Questionnaire and Room Setup

The wise speaker starts gathering information about a speaking gig as soon as the date is set.

As soon as a contract is sent out, it is followed by a Pre-Program Questionnaire as well as Room Setup Preferences. Below is mine.

Client Pre-Program Questionnaire for Dr. Judith Briles

This questionnaire is designed to help Judith prepare for your group so that yours, and your group's expectations will be met. Please take a few moments to fully answer all the questions and return them to our offices when you are finished.

You can mail or email the following requested information. Thank you for your help!

SPECIAL REQUEST:
Please add **Judith@Briles.com** to your email distribution list that pertains to the event that she is speaking for. If you have printed materials on your organization, please forward copies to Judith.

Your Name_____

Organization_____

eMail_____

Phone (work) _____

Phone (cell) _____

Fax_____

Street Address_____

City_____

State_____ Zip _____

Program Date_____

Site Location Address_____

Length of Presentation _____

Expected # of Attendees_____

Percentage of Women _____ Men _____

Meeting Purpose:

1. What are the top three challenges your group/attendees are facing today?

2. What are the three most important things that Judith should know about your group/attendees?

3. Is there any inside information, humor, or "color" that Judith should know about?

4. Are there any topics or subjects that should be avoided?

5. What would you like Judith to accomplish for your group?

6. What professional speakers have you used in the past and what were their topics?

7. If other speakers are on the program, who are they?

8. What will take place immediately before and after Judith's presentation?

9. Do you have any suggestions that will assist Judith in making this the BEST program ever?

Other Resources:
Clients are often interested in supplying one of Judith's books to attendees as a gift to enhance and extend their learning experience after her presentation.

Would you be interested in exploring this option? Yes __ No__

Judith Briles maintains the highest standards of integrity and confidentiality. This information will not be shared without your expressed permission.

Thank you for taking the time to supply this information.

The more prepared Judith is, the better she can serve you.

> ## Thank you for bringing Judith to your group ...

She takes her responsibility to you very seriously ...

We would like to insure the return on your investment of time and money. You can help us do this by following these guidelines:

1. Please have a cordless, hand-held microphone, NO LAVALIERE. If a cordless mike is not available, please provide a cord long enough to allow Judith to walk into the audience for workshops and at least long enough to give her the flexibility to move around on stage for keynotes.

2.   Please have an LCD projector and screen ready. Judith will be using a PowerPoint presentation. She will bring her own laptop plus a backup on a flash drive. It's not uncommon for her to tweak a presentation within hours of the final program.

3.   The presentation she uses will NEVER match the handouts she has sent for duplication. They will be modified. There are multiple copyright issues that she honors.

4.   Take a moment to read Judith's introduction provided by our offices before the actual introduction. When you read it to the audience, please keep it close to the way it was originally written. Verbatim is good!

5.   Have a thermos of hot water on a small table that she can also set up her computer on. No lectern is necessary.

She prefers to stay off of a riser and move around the room, although with large groups, a riser may be necessary.

6. Try to have the group in a "fun" mood before introducing your speaker.
    Sad announcements, moments of silence for a recently-departed friend are appropriate, but not just before introducing the speaker ...

7. For workshops, please provide a flip chart and different colored markers.

8. Judith enjoys and tries to meet as many members of her audience as possible. She will attend your social events if invited (or requested), but please don't make arrangements that require her to be out late at night. She will be in the meeting room at least one hour before her presentation.

9. Please keep in mind that an extended cocktail hour for the audience prior to hearing a speaker is a bad idea. Please save the social beverage events for after the speaker's appearance.

10. If there are awards or extended announcements, either consider having your speaker first, or give the audience a stretch break for a couple of minutes before introducing Judith.

11. Please have only as many chairs as you expect people (with extra chairs stacked up at the back of the room), otherwise, the front rows will be empty.

12. If any doors to the room close loudly, please place door stops appropriately so that the doors will not become a distraction.

13. Please set up any coffee breaks at the back or outside of the meeting room.

This will be less distracting for the participants. Judith will finish within a few minutes of any time frame you give her. At banquets, please serve dessert and coffee, but ask servers to leave clearing and clean-up until after the speaker has presented.

14. Judith will stay at least an entire day of your conference and be available to your attendees. She will also have some of her book titles for a purchasing opportunity. Please have a table dedicated to her for display either by registration or within the main conference room.

15. If the room is rectangular, please have Judith in the middle of the long side.

See Diagrams (following page)

LCD Projector and Laptop will be placed on a 6-foot table, table is "T" to the screen.

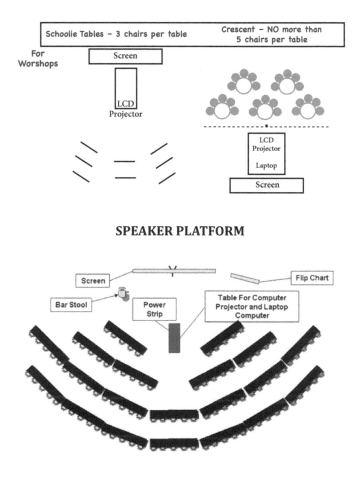

SPEAKER PLATFORM

Starting off with as much information about a group is always a good idea. My Pre-Program Questionnaire started supplying information quickly. Letting your meeting planner know which type of room setup works best for you is helpful. What you want to avoid is the "standard" two wide columns of chairs with the bowling alley in the middle. Ideally you want a "wrap" of chairs around you, keeping the energy in.

**Welcome
to the world of speaking ...
it's a business like
every other business.
Your business has a product: YOU.
You need to sell your product
to the people who want it.**

Part 3:

Ready ... Set ... Go

"Tell me more"
are the magic words
that you want to hear ...

16

Do You Have the Perfect Pitch for Meeting Planners and Book Buyers?

When you know how to Pitch, hooking the listener quickly and succinctly, you get results.

Getting the Speaking Gig is what you want to do. Create a *Call to Action* after your descriptions of your Speaker Info page within your website and/or your Speaker One-Sheet. As you modify your website, this is the blatant "hint" to the meeting planner visitors ... *you are the one* for them and their groups. Some will be a full paragraph, others just a line.

Examples could be:

Book the <u>high-content workplace expert (or YOUR TAGLINE) Sam Speaker (YOUR NAME).</u> He is a crowd-pleasing, life-changing keynote speaker and breakout session leader who adds massive value with every soul-saving strategy he shares. Book him for your next big event. Call 303-555-5555 or email him now to see if he's available for your event: *Sam@GreatSpeaker.com*

———————

Whether she's addressing an intimate group or a standing-room-only crowd, count on international and career-changing speaker and overcoming-adversity graduate Sarah Johanson to inspire your audience members to acknowledge their successes, recognize their pitfalls, and open the door for the opportunities coming their way.

Call 303-555-5555 or email her now to see if she's available for your event: *Sarah@GreatSpeaker.com*

If your members are challenged with low morale and decreased productivity in their workplaces, using my 5-Step Morph the Workplace workshop will turn work into a joy.

———————

Caring for an aging relative can suck the energy out of the caregiver. My three steps to transform dread-giving to loving caregiving will be celebrated by receiver and giver.

———————

If you want to get your kids to enthusiastically put down their electronic gadgets, my-easy-to-use concepts to rejoin the family will have them asking, "Can we do this again?"

————————

Calls to Action are necessary. Otherwise, most sit on their duffs. What's essential for you to know are key words within the industry, company, or association. And, of course, what the pain points are that you can solve. These are your pitch points. Write them up.

For Authors in Pitching Books ...

Each year, I host two events that require authors to pitch their book.

Every January, I organize the *PublishingAtSea.com* conference. Seven days at sea in the Caribbean where we play, have workshops, and get our marketing mojos revved up. Cruising days are workshop days and the cruise line lets me offer Books at Sea—within a two-hour slot, attendees with books are in the main area where passengers drop in and buy books. Fast pitches and fun interaction.

Every October, I host my annual Author's Tea ... a Saturday afternoon where up to 15 authors get the opportunity to pitch their books in 60 seconds or less to approximately 100+ book-buying attendees—my invited friends and all of the authors' invited friends, too.

It's a stand-up-and-sit-down tea with the usual food spread one would find at a High Tea— mini-sandwiches and cheeses, plus a variety of yummy desserts. The event is held in my home. And, of course, there are a variety of teas to choose from. Yes, I roll up my sleeves and bake, cook, assemble and put on a full spread for all attendees. The energy is always fun (one year it was on Halloween afternoon and many of the authors showed up in costume). It's a great networking and schmoozing event. Lots of books are sold ... providing gifts for brother Charlie, Aunt Sue, kids, best friends and for

self for the holidays just around the corner.
All ages are welcome.

The authors get the book sales and pay me $25
to participate to cover some of the food costs.
I view it as a book marketing coop ... one of the
strings attached around being a featured author
is committing to bring at least four guests to
the tea as well. As I've told my participants,
"It doesn't matter if your guests already own
your book ... in fact, they become cheerleaders
for you—your Super Fans telling other guests
how wonderful your book is. It's the fabulous
word-of-mouth marketing in action.

> *The concept of
> being "concise" doesn't register
> in the response.*

From the get-go, featured authors are told to
keep their pitch short—the shorter, the better.
It's always a challenge. Keep in mind: When

anyone rambles, listeners' ears start closing. Savvy authors who want to sell books learn how to pitch—with a hook that gets the listener to think, to say ... "tell me more." That "tell me more" could be in an open Q & A, and in the case of the Author's Tea, it becomes the opportunity to talk directly with the author in an environment that is comfortable and casual.

I give my tea authors 60 seconds to pitch, to start the connection process. Since I usually have a new book each year, I'm one of the pitchers—I can do it in 10 seconds. What about you?

When someone asks you what you speak about or what your book is about, can you clearly and concisely say it in 15 seconds or less? Most fail miserably at this essential task. When his or her mouth opens, words flow ... and flow ... and flow. Sometimes, they can become an endless river. They ramble on about the background; why the book was written or why they speak;

how the book solves all the problems of the disease, the situation, you name it. The concept of being "concise" doesn't register in the response. It should.

Around you are the voices of thousands of people competing for space in the speaker market and reader's head. Learn how to get your voice, your expertise heard above the clatter and racket of the crowd.

> *You will be life-changing for those who hear you.*

You want your pitch to create one response from the listener: Tell me more. The listener may think it; he or she may say it. Your pitch needs to elicit it.

Acquiring the skills for pitching yourself, you will discover that the results adapt to publicity and marketing, as well as anyone else who lands in your path.

Within your pitch, use one or more of these elements:

1. Your words should create an instant visual;

2. Your words need to be succinct;

3. Your words can be quirky and fun;

4. Your words can include something familiar;

5. Your words can have a rhyme and rhythm to them; or

6. Your words can use alliteration.

Both speakers and authors are notorious when it comes to talking about their expertise and books ... or trying to describe what they are about in just a few seconds. When you know how to Pitch, hooking the listener quickly and succinctly, you get results. "Tell me more about ..." becomes the response—you have thrown the lure out—the portal is now open to engage the potential buyer of your services and reel him or her in.

Create your "call to action" ... most likely, it will be part of the pitch that will bring the meeting planner to you.

The result: You will be life-changing for those who hear you. And you will sell books at every gig. I guarantee it.

To get your head around creating a one-sentence pitch—pick up a copy of the **New York Times** *and study the Book Reviews section. Each title has a one-line description—often under 10 words. One of my favorites was for a kid's book titled* **The Day the Crayons Quit** *by Drew Daywalt. The description: "Colorful problems arise when Duncan's crayons revolt."*

Speakers are "connectors" ...
they need to connect with
their audience from the get-go ...
and they need to weave their
ideas and takeaways with
elements that their listeners
will connect with.

17

Engaging Your Audience

*Think the five senses: seeing, hearing, smelling,
feeling, and touching.*

Boring speeches suck, pure and simple. The last
thing you should do is stand behind a lectern
and just talk—worse yet, read what you wrote.
Now, if you have a physical limitation, you may
be limited in movement on a stage. Other than

that, you need to pepper your talk. Think the five senses: seeing, hearing, smelling, feeling, and touching. You can have actual visuals that display any one of them, but so can descriptive words. But for me, visuals are essential.

*You are on ...
before you are on!*

With the statement that visuals don't have to be slides or videos, think about it. They are so much more. You can roll them out with your verbal descriptions. Wonderful colors that can be used in a kaleidoscope of landscapes; noises that produce calm, fear and amusement; odors that are exotic, comforting, or cause disgust; emotions that can trigger an array of feelings; and touching with breezes, impact even one's lips.

Prepping for the Stage

Before I took the stage, I always asked my introducer or the planner what they wanted me to do after I closed. Turn to give the mic to someone (who?), tell the members to go to lunch ... what?

And, I always donated a percentage of my book sales to the group. I never pitched them from the stage. I would remind the introducer that I was doing so and asked her to let the group know that I would be available the rest of the conference to answer any questions they might have.

Consistently, the introducer reminded the audience to visit me at my book table and that a percentage of sales was being donated to their foundation, scholarship, etc.

When I know the introducer was getting close to starting, it was time to do a health break. Do it. Check your teeth also and hair, too. For women, add a touch of lipstick. I would shake my feet and arms; take deep breaths; and yawn. And I would not be sitting in the front row or at a table. Get up. Move to the side. And start smiling if you haven't been. Members of the audience are already watching you. You are on … before you are on!

Openings and Closings

Your *opening* sets the stage. You need to grab the audience. Do not … do not … waste an audience's time and thank everyone but your uncle for bringing you there. Don't comment about your travel and pick up at the airport UNLESS it's part of your opening story. DO get started. You are on. Begin with a humorous or poignant story or even a dramatic one; then wrap it around your theme/topic. You could add an amazing statistic that ties to the topic or a quote that is relevant … but come out strong. Your opening story is usually identified as a signature story—it's yours, you are directly involved in it.

You will then move into the structure of your presentation and key points.

Your *closing* is the ribbon that wraps it all up. Sometimes it's a summary of key points and then hooked to something personal that you hadn't revealed in your quest of the topic. Whatever it is, it needs power. When you end your speech, you can leave them laughing; you can leave them crying; or you can leave them thinking. But, you can't just leave them.

What about Q & A?

My preference is: don't. When you are on a roll, you don't want to be halted to take questions from the audience and reduce your energy and flow. It will happen. If your planner-host-sponsor desires you to do one, I suggest you hold your last point, then come back to it and then deliver your close.

In a keynote, in most cases, there won't be a
Q & A. If one is required, I would say something
like:

> Before I make my last point and close, we've
> allocated a few minutes for your questions.
> In speaking with many of you prior to my
> presentation, this question repeatedly was
> asked. I'll share it with all of you now and
> then take additional questions.

Here's what happens in most Q & As. Unless
cards of some sort were passed out to gather
questions, you may have the deer-in-the-
headlights look in front of you. Those who have
questions are hoping someone else will ask
them. By you throwing out the first one (even
if no one asked you one—that's a fudge line
I used), you loosen the group up a bit and a
few brave attendees will then ask questions.

Now, go back to your final point and close.

Stories—Yours, Not Someone Else's

Often called "signature stories," they can be funny, emotional, moving, sad—you name it, they are ideal to weave within your presentation.

Yours can come from childhood to adulthood. They can come from family members or observations. In person; at the movies; at an event; on TV ... the world is your oyster—all it needs is your participation and reaction.

> *Stories are used as setups and illustrations. They are used to connect with your audience.*

What makes them unique is that you experienced them ... and, that you didn't pick them up when you heard someone else tell them.

I have stories that tie into my key points in presentations. I have stories I use for opening speeches and for closing them. *They are my stories*—not someone else's.

They range from utter humility (my underwear dropped down at a gig); to doing dumb things (I smacked my head on the butt of an elephant when I wasn't paying attention); to discovering a stash of $30,000 in an overstuffed chair (a casual comment made by a new client as I visited her in her home); to my son cornering me on a chairlift wanting to know what money we had (which led to the structure of how I taught my kids about money); to many more. All real. All happened to me. All cover the range of the senses.

When I've had repeated engagements, it's not uncommon for attendees to ask/request that I tell a favorite story again. And I do.

My stories are used as setups and illustrations. They are used to connect with my audience. If I had a predominately female one, the underwear story is always a hit and the perfect setup to make me a real person, to laugh a lot, and to make a key point.

> *Make it a practice to study other speakers.*

Early in my speaking career, I was only speaking about personal finance. The underwear incident happened early in my career; the elephant story when I was in my mid-20s; how I showed signs of being a writer and speaker when I was seven years old; talking to my kids about money came about in my late 30s; the overstuffed chair happened in my late 20s—note the age range.

When I transitioned to conflict management and toxic behavior in the female-dominated workplace, my experiences from the survival of an embezzlement and a variety of personal traumas I underwent became rich material for my speaking.

As an author for over 40 years, my DNA has morphed into publishing related stories that just keep coming to me.

I don't need other people's stories ... and neither do you.

As a speaker, your stories and storytelling are the unique gems that separate you from others. *Make it a practice to study other speakers.* Where do they insert their stories? What kind of stories are they? How does the audience react?

Now look at the presentation you currently have or one that you are creating. Where can you use stories to enhance a point or illustrate a thought? What story in your life can you use as a setup to what your talk is about?

You are richer because of your stories, and so will be your audience when you share them.

Storytelling Aha:
The more you tell your stories,
the better your delivery will get.

Use Your Stories for Openings, Closings, and to Reinforce Key Points

1. The "Why I'm Here" Story

It's all about the emotional side of why you are speaking and sharing your story, your expertise, your whatever ...

2. The Elephant in the Room

There's usually one ... or more ... in any group. With your skill as a speaker, you should be able to "pull from your bag of experiences (and tricks)" and morph a situation or to draw out a situation. Sometimes, you may use an "Imagine this ...." or even a one-on-one with an audience member.

3. The Example Story

It can be yours or a story you've heard. For example ...

Sometimes stories are OPS—other people's stories; sometimes a myth or fable or a kid's story that will connect with your point. As you construct your stories ...

■ Usually, it's best to keep your story brief: two to three minutes.

■ Know *WHY* you are telling the story—is it to set the stage of your overall message? A point within it?

■ Find stories from your own life—personal stories reflect your authenticity.

■ Do you have a "hero"?

■ If your story is about a "beef," make sure that it ties to a problem that can be connected with your theme and has a solution. Your listeners need resolution and closure.

■ Emotion counts. Your emotional involvement with your story—fear, anger, frustration, excitement, joy—triggers your listeners.

■ True stories about people carry more clout than made-up stories.

■ Ends well. Don't leave your listeners in a downer mood—end it on an upbeat note.

■ Don't be preachy—let your audience members draw their own conclusions.

Storytelling Aha: The more you tell your stories, the better your delivery.

TV and Movies Are Terrific Resources

Are you a TV snob? I hope not. Television may well be the secret sauce to connect with your audience. Why? Because the majority watches favorite shows. When you niche yourself, you want to deep-dive into identifying the top shows. When I worked within health care, it wasn't difficult to know that my audiences watched *ER, Grey's Anatomy, House, St. Elsewhere* and *Nurse Jackie.* I watched them, too. In my presentations, I would use scenes to illustrate and support points. My audience was with me.

What shows are your audiences—your crowd watching? When I worked within the healthcare field, I Googled "top medical TV shows" and "most popular TV medical dramas." If I did it now, shows like *Chicago Med* and *The Good Doctor* would have joined the ranks. It's your turn: Using the phrases "what are the top or most popular TV shows on your topic," see what pops up.

How about movies? Depending on what you like and view, what scenes and/or story lines could tie to your message? When I presented my Zapping Conflict and How to Deal with Pit Bulls with Lipstick programs, I always included a module on Unwritten Rules. I would segue to a scene from the movie, *A Team of Their Own*. As I began to roll it out, I noticed my audience immediately paying attention, leaning forward, maybe wondering what I was going to do with it. When I was ready to throw a question to them, they had the answer and repeated in unison lines back at me ... verbatim from the movie. I made my point; they got it; and remembered it. And we had a good laugh when it occurred. I had linked it to something they were familiar with.

The tip is to use something familiar when you can. Those in your audience watch TV, view movies, attend sporting events and concerts. Using a key scene, a well-known phrase, or a running story within a series can enrich your presentations and the ability of your audience to take away your message.

Creating Activities and Exercises

Trainers and workshop leaders typically use activities and exercises to make points, to create breaks in their narrative and to energize a group.

Ideally, for both you and your participants, they will be sprinkled throughout your format. Some may involve physical movement; some group involvement; and some individual work.

Always act with a goal in mind. As a speaker and facilitator, use a combo of seriousness and fun.

If you are doing an all-day event, afternoons can drag out. As soon as lunch is over and depending on what was served (defer any desserts to later in the afternoon), you usually have to work harder to maintain your audience's attention. Activities that are group-oriented always reenergize a group.

When I did all-day workshops, I never went more than 70 minutes without doing something that required the group to get up, move around, and do something. It moves your day forward and gives them a break from sitting. And, it gives you a few minutes as well.

Creating Slides That Engage

At every conference I've attended as a participant and every conference where I've been a speaker, there has not been a time when a presenter hasn't put the audience through PowerPoint hell in some way.

Slides have been downright ugly; impossible to read; way too much material (words) on them; none of the techie add-ons work; videos embedded don't work; and slide color is an eyesore. I started listing them and created a PowerPoint Boo-Boo list.

20 PowerPoint Boo-Boos

#1 **The slides are too-too**
The font is too stylized. The contrast with slide color and words doesn't mesh. The slides are too detailed.

#2 **The speaker apologizes for them from the stage**
Then don't use them!

#3 **The colors are awful**
Contrast is important, but too bright can hurt eyes, irritate audience.

#4 The font size is too small
No one should have to squint from anywhere in the room. Minimal size is a 28-point font.

#5 Using detailed charts and graphs
Don't ... unless everyone has a printed copy in hand.

#6 Audience members can't read the font
Use a sans-serif and don't use more than two or three fonts. Avoid any shadows and most borders.

#7 The background is the wrong color
Either dark or the very light is best— print should be opposite. Don't use red— ever.

#8 The letter/word color is wrong
Use a contrast, so words pop, and there is no question what the words are.

#9 Slides are too complicated ... keep them simple

Key phrases, simple sentences only. Don't overload content. Sometimes just ONE word will do it.

#10 Slides should be consistent

Use a master format to create a consistent look. Make sure you add a © and your name on each slide.

#11 Animation doesn't work

Sometimes it does, sometimes it doesn't—don't risk it.

#12 Audio doesn't work

Sometimes it does, sometimes it doesn't. You are the best audio.

#13 Poor use of cartoons

They should be understandable, READ them out loud with "tone." People read at different rates—keep them on track with your voice.

#14 PowerPoint is out of control
Don't use all the bells and whistles available just because you can.

#15 Including all your slides in a handout!
Don't. Ever. This is your intellectual property.

#16 Not having a handout of any of the slides
Modify your handouts; include some of yours, but not all. Delete cartoons.

#17 Handout is impossible to read
Print handout in grayscale and multiple slides per page. Caution—If you are duplicating your slides in the handout, are they readable? Up to four slides on a page usually works. If your intent is for participants to write notes, use the three-slides format that includes lines beside each slide.

#18 Computer or Tablet goes to sleep before you start

It's smart to boot everything up and be ready to go ... and then your computer goes into hibernation—put a blank slide in BEFORE your presentation starts so you can click on it for a wake-up call.

#19 Not carrying your own computer

Sure, everyone has one ... but you may want to make last-minute changes to your program. And don't forget your power source—I actually carry a spare (they do die).

#20 Not having a copy of your presentation on a flash drive

For "just in case." Refer back to #19—I did forget my power source, leaving it plugged in at my office. Because I had my presentation on the flash drive, my host had a laptop on site (as half the room did).

Always Incorporate Humor ...
No Matter How Serious Your Topic Is

As a nonfiction writer, my topics of personal finance, conflict resolution, dealing with toxic behaviors, dealing with failure and overcoming adversity, and how to publish would not be viewed as knee-slappers. Yet, in every workshop or keynote I deliver, I use humor. You have to as well.

Yes, boring speeches are the pits, orally and visually. For me, being a speaker, as well as an author, is an honor and a privilege. You will earn your place on the platform. It will take some time and a lot of practice. It's how you get better.

I learned quickly that there were audiences that were better suited for me. You will discover, to your delight, when their needs, their attitude, their appreciation of you are the right fit.

And always remember, when you end your speech, you can leave your audience laughing; you can leave them crying; or you can leave them thinking. But never can you just leave them.

18

Crafting Your Keynote Speech or Workshop

*Every speech has beginning and an end ...
and a structure.*

JUDITH BRILES, OTHEBOOKSHEPHERD.COM

Of course, you want to be good ... in fact, how about exceptional and a speaker that gets you invited back as well as referred to others? One of the truths that those who have been on the platform for many years have is a consistency about them. They are consistently good. They can be counted on to deliver what they promise. They leave their audiences with nuggets to chew on and new tools to implement in their workplaces and lives.

> *Counting my books sold at events, it was common to double my original speaking fee.*

There are many, many speakers who are more skilled than I am; who made more money per speech than I did; and had far more booking dates a year than I had. Let's be real. If you are going to model yourself after someone, is it the right model? There was no way I wanted to be on the road 200 days a year; nor did I speak to the corporate market or the industries/ associations that paid the big bucks. And, I was a female—surprise, surprise, we made good money—but 95 percent of the time, it was the guys who pulled down the mega bucks—those hefty five-figure speaking fees.

The speaking fee I made via presenting at nursing associations and at hospital programs averaged $5,000. Counting my books sold at events, it was common to double my original speaking fee. I was happy with my results. And, I was away from home approximately half the year.

On an ongoing basis, I tweaked my presentations; added new ones; and kept on writing books. Because I was "out there," I was in touch with the needs of my audience and what I published and spoke to them about.

Every speech has a beginning and an end ... and a structure. Let's start with your structure.

Your Structure

Question: What is your talk about?

_____

_____

*Next question: What's the premise and objective
of your talk in one sentence? This is the "why."*

_____

_____

Understanding exactly what your talk is about
and the foundation of it along with the premise
and objective for your audience are essential in
hitting the homeruns in your speaking career.

Think of your speech as a sandwich. The bread
on each side holds it together. That's your
Opening and Closing. In between is the main
ingredient—the meat—with a variety of

complements to take away the dryness; and others to add a touch of crunch and spice and delicious flavors. The main ingredient is a combo of your premise and objective. The complements introduce your key points, stories, research, statistics, exercises, and advice.

The layout of the speech will look like this:

1. *Opening to "set" message theme*

2. *Points of wisdom*
    (5-10 minutes for each point)

    - Point
    - Stories, or
    - Examples, or
    - Suggestions, or
    - Advice
    - Repeat Point
    - Move to next Point

3. *Q & A (maybe) ... Before I close, are there any questions?*

4. *Closing*

Your Beginning

How will you start your presentation—and with what? Is it a story; a statistic; a reference; a quotation? Will it have humor? Drama? Suspense? Will you leave it opened up and then loop back to your opening story at the end of your talk? Figure it out and then practice, practice, practice.

Your Closing

Your wrap-up brings it all together. Another story? A revelation? A recap of your key points, then what? A call to action? What? Figure it out and then practice, practice, practice.

Speaking Resources

I'm a huge fan of TED ... as in **TED Talks** ... From 6 to 18 minutes, individuals from anywhere and everywhere; with an unbelievable range of ideas and expertise "do their thing." A TED presentation is highly crafted. Emotional. Insightful. Revealing. All in just a few minutes.

Take the time to study several. How do they open? How do they close? What are they weaving in between the opening and closing in just a few minutes?

What you will quickly discover is that presenters on the TED stage don't waste time. They don't ramble. They get to the "meat" of what they came to share and they do it quickly.

The main website is *TED.com* ... you can find the most recent and the most watched. YouTube is another option to search topics and talks.

Discover **Toastmasters International**. It has approximately 16,000 clubs in more than 140 countries. Helpful and always loaded with tips for speakers at all levels, it's objective is to empower individuals to become more effective communicators and leaders. Explore its website at Toastmasters.org to find a club near you.

Membership groups like the **National Speakers Association** with 37 chapters in the US have a variety of programs for speakers at multiple levels. When I lived in California, I was president of the Northern California NSA chapter and later served on the national NSA board and chaired one of its national workshops. Explore its website *NSASpeaker.org* to find a chapter near you.

Twice a year, I deliver **Judith Briles Speaking Unplugged** in Denver, Colorado. Attendees come to me for an intensive two-day highly interactive coaching program that includes "hot-seats" for each participant in March or November. Unplugged is limited to 25 participants so I can customize for participants and deliver one-on-one attention. Explore my website, *TheBookShepherd.com*, for details and schedule under the Events tab.

Once you get your head around the "why" of your talk; what your key points are; what you will use to support each; and how you want to open and close ... you are on your way. If you ever get into a time crunch and you need to reduce, you can cut out one of your "points" and story, stats, activity/exercise, etc., that goes with it. Ten minutes or more can be knocked off quickly.

When you speak, you have the opportunity to deliver a miracle. How powerful is that? Those who hear you can experience a different world;

a different take; view their life differently ... and be different. Yes, you can deliver a miracle. What an opportunity. What a responsibility.

I thank you and so will your audiences.

> *Your keynote presentation will have three key elements: Opening, Points of wisdom with supporting info, and Closing.*

19

Marketing Yourself for Booking Success

You have a product to market. That product is you and your speech.

Most speakers are the main marketers for their services. Speakers are usually soloists, handling everything—from marketing to travel to performer. Others have help—a marketing assistant, a travel agent—and the speaker simply shows up to perform. Some work with speaking agents who, in a way, are marketers and take a percentage of the negotiated speaking fee, but they are in the minority.

What are you doing to position yourself and your expertise to the right markets?

- Are you coattailing what your competitors are doing?

- Are you using every conceivable word or phrase that might bring buyers to you?

- Are you a master at "BB Gun Marketing"?

Do the words you use really, really narrow in on your expertise ... or are you positioning yourself as a generalist, using every conceivable word?

Are you making yourself findable to the meeting planners who are looking for someone like you ... not just anyone?

> *Oh-oh, it's an OMG moment for sure!*

For this year, I encourage you to focus on *what you do and what your expertise is versus what you think every potential meeting planner—your primary buyer—needs.*

The truth is: *Being a good speaker is important ... but it does not guarantee that you will be sought after or make a lot of money.* And being an expert doesn't guarantee that you are a good speaker or that a group will fork over big bucks to hear you. Oh-oh, it's an OMG moment for sure!

So ... what separates you from the pack? Let's say you are "that expert" and you are a "good speaker." Getting speaking engagements is a business. You have a product to market. That product is you and your talk.

When you just "speak" ... anywhere for anything, the odds are that you will be so-so. There's no niching in play; whether there is true expertise bubbling could be questionable—you just may like to speak. Repeat business comes from "memorable moments" ... those ahas and take-aways that audience members hang onto and share; those ideas that are usable and make a difference; those ideas that offer solutions to problems and pain they are experiencing.

The truth is: *Marketing can be exhausting for most,* especially when a speaker is not focused and practicing BB Gun Marketing to any and all. When you have a niche market approach, it's so much easier and can be fun. Over the 30-plus years I was on the road as a full-time speaker, my marketing was broken into two categories:

On the road—I was at conferences and private groups where my niche was. I hung out; I interacted with attendees when I wasn't speaking. Referrals came.

In the office—every morning, I dedicated ONE to TWO HOURS to marketing ... only. I followed up. I made phone calls. I sent notes. I send postcards. Info was entered into my office database with follow-up dates to repeat the process. Then I went about my day, turning over to my assistant what she needed to follow up.

The truth is: *You need to stay in front of your audience.* That's what blogs, podcasts, newsletters, ezines, social media, and media are for. You want to become a content provider—supporting your expertise and your persona.

The truth is: *You need more than one talk.*
At least today, you do. If you are a keynoter only,
create a few. If you do trainings and workshops,
have multiple. And create multiple titles for the
same workshop, training, or keynote. Titles are
"pulls"—what attracts one planner may not
attract another. For authors, one of your titles
should be your book title as well.

The truth is: *You need to think beyond one
book—books breed more books.* Once you
have fans and followers, they want more. Think
spin-off products. Yup, from pen giveaways,
bookmark "tools," wristbands, shirts, online
courses, webinars, and other items that can be
free and for sale. My high-end nail files were free
at my events and disappeared when I brought
them out, and so were the buttons I created to
support a new book. When I showed up at one
nursing conference with purple T-shirts that
proclaimed I'm a *Nurse of Confidence ... Beware
...* wowsa, they jumped at paying $15 and 200
disappeared quickly one afternoon.

The truth is: *You are a problem solver.* I've said this throughout *How to Create a $1,000,000 Speech.* And I'm saying it again here. It doesn't matter if you are a humorist or storyteller ... you deliver entertainment ... your listener wants relief and escape—it's their problem and you will solve it. For the topic speaker—be it health, how-to, business, etc.—whatever the issues and problems are, you step up with strategies to lessen or remove them.

How cool is it to be able to share your gifts? Very cool, I think.

*What motivates your buyer—
the meeting planner?*

Here Are 4 Essential Questions for Your Speaking Marketing Success

Every year, Groundhog Day pops up—a silly holiday that is supposed to predict the weather climate for the next six weeks. Punxsutawney Phil emerges in the AM of February 2nd and does his thing. We find out later if he sees his shadow or not. According to Groundhog Day followers, winter will continue for another six weeks if he sees his shadow. If the shadow is nonexistent, it means that spring will come sooner. Now, according to the arrival of the Winter Solstice in December, it will continue until the Spring Equinox, usually the third week in March. More likely, it's seven weeks—but what's a few days?

If the shadow shows, many view it as the opportunity to stay in. Spring and the new work it brings are still far away. But is it? And should you be thinking that way? In other words, do you stay in the shadows of your marketing, waiting for a better day? Don't.

The better thing to do is ask yourself a question:

What motivates you as a speaker?

It's a question every speaker needs to ask and answer. Is it a simple "I did it"? Or, is it something else? Whatever it is for you, it should be the guide of what you do and how you do it.

Your next question is:

What motivates your buyer—
the meeting planner?

You and your speech are products. Any product sold today has "motivation" behind it—I don't care if it's an air-conditioner, new car, comfy sweater, a new restaurant ... whatever. If it is looking for a consumer to buy it, it's a product. The marketing team is probing, searching, and studying its consumer. The team doesn't jump into it lightly. Then it creates a plan designed to lure you, hook you, and create a sale. You and your quest to book a gig are no different.

My next question is:

What's your marketing plan?

The truth is no one is going to motivate you to take any action in creating your marketing plan and launching it. YOU must be the motivator. You must be the decision maker. You must launch it for your author and book success.

And, if you don't like the results you are currently experiencing, I arrive at my final question:

What are you going to do to change them?

The bottom line is this: Depending on your topic and which groups would be attracted to it, you need to be reaching out.

- Identify when annual meetings and conferences are held.

- Check out website for info—are there speakers?

- Who decides on which speakers and programs?

- How much planning time is needed?

- Include, as part of your fee, the ability to sell your books.

- Take credit cards, checks, and cash. If you are comfortable, sometimes an IOU.

- Ask your host if the attendees are a book-buying group.

- Bring books for about a third of the crowd.

- If it's local, always carry a few cartons of books in your car.

- If speaking at an event whose participants come from the area, contact the local bookstore.

Social Media and Your Marketing

When it comes to social media, this is the time to KISP—Keep It Simple Please. You don't need a PhD in social media to grasp the basics. I'm not going to go into the how-tos of tweeting,

Facebook ads, or posting on Instagram. What I want to share are common-sense tactics.

1. *Determine which platforms your buyers and fans use.* For business and many nonfiction books, it will be LinkedIn, so creating a LinkedIn Group and Twitter will most likely be on your radar. This is where you need to start asking, including any meeting planners you come into contact with. What do they like? What do they use? Is there a favorite group they belong to?

2. *Post, Post, Post.* It's that simple. And do it daily. Remember, you are providing content. This is not the time to virtually jump up and down while shouting, "Look at me, look at me." Promote and recommend others in your social media streams. Experts share and cross-promote.

   Your posts should be relevant and interesting. You can also have a little fun.

I would caution you to step away from anything political, religious (unless you are speaking within these markets), or gossipy. Your goal is to be viewed as a reliable guide and someone who followers want to pay attention to.

Use a social media management tool like Hootsuite to manage your time and retain your sanity.

3. *Give away free info.* Yes, you charge for your speaking services. But seed your brilliance with articles, blogs, webinars, even speeches or workshops that are totally free. Articles and blogs are easy to do as is a webinar. Donating a few speeches and workshops each year makes sense. People are there. They hear you. They experience you. Your info; your wisdom; being at an event—whether it's someone else's or your own—you will be noticed. And, because you've "seeded" the

groundwork, meeting planners know that you will be an attraction.

4. *Don't forget to include some type of Call to Action.* Pose a question at the end of a post. Invite your followers to email you for a free copy of something. Offer a free 15-minute strategy session on your expertise.

If you have questions about any tools that social media offers, my favorite website is *SocialMediaExaminer.com.* It's clear, concise and offers step-by-step how-tos for just about anything. Subscribe to its blogs.

What Meeting Planners Want to Know

The odds are, there are many experts in your field. You should know who the top ones are (outside of you, of course); subscribe to their blogs and follow their social media posts. This is part of your homework, PLUS it will keep you current in changes that you might not be aware of.

The questions you need to keep in front of you are:

> *Why should a planner hire you versus someone else?*
> *What makes you special?*

Start with your own story ... Are you a celebrity? Survived a disaster? Experienced an unbelievable traumatic situation? Experienced an event that changed your life? In other words, what brings you to your expertise?

Walk your talk ... talk your walk ... and model both.

Reveal any business experience ... Have you turned a company around? Have you lost it all and started over, building a new company? Were you an essential employee, manager, or leader in a high-profile company? Did you invent something that took off?

Share a unique method ... Losing weight; stop smoking; solving a health issue; built a business around it; sold a million books about your technique; etc.

Your style ... Meeting planners want to know if you are interactive; are you a comic or do you use humor; do you have a talent that you incorporate such as singing, dancing, use unusual props or magic; do you use slides; or, do you just lecture?

What you bring to the attendees ... How will you help them. And will you show them how to achieve their goals? The only way to know what the meeting planner is looking for is to ask. Then, based on your experience, speak to what he or she needs.

Reaching Out ... My Method with Phones and Postcards

Over 200 billion emails are sent out each day. Add that to the over six billion text messages created daily and then mix those with one billion Facebook posts; 500 million tweets; and 95 million pictures on Instagram daily. That's a bit of an overwhelm, don't you think? What can you do to get the attention of a meeting planner?

It's easy to get lost in the onslaught of communication possibilities. I'm going to suggest TWO old-fashioned ways to connect with a meeting planner:

Your telephone · Snail mail

Before you think I've lost it, think again. Does it take more work to make a phone call ... and to follow up multiple times before you might connect? Yes, it does. But my years of experience demonstrate that it's highly successful.

Think about snail mail. How much do you get in your mail box? Is it more or less than before email became the norm? I bet it's less—much less. Where email can easily go to a "spam" file; get deleted; get blocked from a filter system or just go unopened; a snail mail piece means that someone—hopefully who it was addressed to—physically touches it. The reality is, first-class mail has dropped by 40 percent since the year 2000. In 2000, the US Postal Service reported that 103 million pieces were delivered. In 2016, that number dropped to 61 million first-class pieces.

In other words, the competition is less in getting someone's attention. Think about it—less junk mail to compete with. That's significant in my book!

For me, in most cases, it took six to eight times before I got a real commitment or a pass, even with those who had already said, "I want you." I would leave short messages, each varied, on voice mail. People are busy—remember all those emails, etc., that they are bombarded with.

Then I would follow up with a postcard, a picture of my book cover on one side. On the other side, a message about what I could bring to the group—all done by the printer. I always made sure a small space was allotted so I could write a short, personalized note. While I was listening to the voice mail message, I was already handwriting the addressee's name and address on the postcard. I would leave my message, finish the postcard, and make a notation of what I did in my customer management system (I used ACT!), with a callback scheduled a week later. And then I proceeded with my next call.

Why would you want to be lost in a sea of mega-millions?

Remember, I spent one to two hours in the early AM making my marketing calls when I was in the office (about 10 days a month). That time frame included addressing and jotting notes on the postcards. When my marketing time was up, I immediately headed to the mailbox and deposited all of the postcards generated for the day.

That's what I did. I reached out. I left a message on voice mail when I didn't get the person I was calling. I wrote out a postcard and mailed it. I started the connection. I followed up week after week until a decision was made. Do you realize how different that is? Why would you want to be lost in a sea of mega-millions?

The majority of meeting planners are women. Women are more relationship-oriented than men are. Planners want to engage with speakers they have seen; been referred to; or have thoroughly checked out. It's their business. They want to work with individuals with whom they can build trust, who will work with their audience, and who will make them look good for bringing you in.

I didn't start out pitching myself when I got a "live" person. I found something to personalize the call—that's when you should check out the social media profile of whoever you are calling or something on the company website. If I had already met the person, I may have noted an item on a business card that I could later refer to.

Here's what I suggest you do if you don't know the planner or decision maker:

1. Call. Keep it very short. If you were referred to her, say by whom. If you get voice mail, leave a short message.

2. Send a postcard and schedule another call in a week.

3. Send an email with a "tidbit" in the message that you thought might be

useful—something about the industry; a news item that could have an impact; maybe something that just is pleasant or meaningful. Again, keep it short.

4. Repeat.

Here's what I suggest you do if you have already met the planner or decision maker:

1. Call. Remind her of where you met and the reason why you are calling. If she had asked you to hold a date, include it. Keep it very short. If you get voice mail, leave a message.

2. Send a postcard and schedule another call in a week.

3. Send an email with a "tidbit" in the message that you thought might be useful— something about the industry; a news item that could have an impact; maybe something that just is pleasant or meaningful. Again, keep it short.

4. Repeat.

My results? I was booked at least a year out. Over a 35-year period, I have earned in excess of $3,000,000 in speaking fees and generated more than $2,000,000 in book sales. It was lots of phone calls and lots of postcards that generated and supported my business!

Creating Specials

When I had a new book (which meant a new presentation), I often did a deal ... and I did it via snail mail and mailed it to everyone on my mailing list. Creating a one-page flyer, I would come up with a catchy headline and offer my speaking services at half my fee for the first ten people who committed. Every time I did it, in less than a week, all ten "deals" were taken. I knew from my book-selling history that my onsite sales would at least double the reduced fee. What this did was create the buzz for the new book, speech, and me.

When anyone called me after the first ten slots were filled, I always suggested, "Let's work something out ... who do you know that knows about me, needs a speaker for an event, and is within a reasonable driving range (any direction/possibly another state)? If I can pull three of you together within a 200-mile radius within the same week, I'll discount all of you." And more gigs were contracted for.

It became a win for my caller; a win for her contacts; and a win for me.

Speaking Local and Going National

For me, there was no glory in the hometown. I would have loved to speak more in my home state. It was a rare occasion. It's how I accumulated in excess of 2,000,000 miles on airlines. Start local ... it may be where you begin and get your feet wet.

There are plenty of organizations out there who are looking for "freebie" speakers—think Rotary,

Lions, chambers of commerce (men's and women's), Junior Leagues, libraries—there are dozens of places to reach out to. In my *Judith Briles Speaking Unplugged* event, I give all attendees a list with 80 types of groups to reach out to.

Go National … you don't need to be a bestselling author or high-profile personality to be hired. What planners want is content. Do you have it? When you are at an event, offer a freebie to your audience. Tell them what it is and pass a basket for their business cards or ask them to email you. Then contact those who share or reach out promptly.

Do ask: *Do you belong to a group or does your company bring in speakers? Or, do you know of a group (or company or organization or association) that you think might appreciate being contacted regarding my speaking topic/services?*

There is no one way to market yourself. Each group and organization you reach out to will be different. What you need is some flexibility in your bag of marketing tools, recognizing that some groups and meeting planners need more hand-holding; more personal contact and different types of information to form their decision. *Be prepared* should be your motto. Show up should be your practice—online and in-person.

Walk your talk ... talk your walk ... and model both. If you speak on health, you shouldn't look unwell and in poor fitness. If you speak on parenting, yet you've never been in the trenches of being one, are you really a fit? If you speak on balance and yet your life is in turmoil, what model are you?

> *REMEMBER:*
> *Walk your talk ...*
> *talk your walk ...*
> *and model both.*

Sponsors are partners.
They support you with promotion
and moneys. You support them with
acknowledgment from the stage
or within media interviews,
materials given to audiences,
and other agreed upon items.

20

Is There a Sponsor in Your Midst?

Getting a Sponsor for Your Platform

My first sponsorship started with a phone call from a colleague in New York. I was asked, "Would you be interested in being a spokesperson for a product? This company is looking for a woman who knows how to speak, has written a book, and has dealt with adversity."

This had my name all over it. "What's the company ... and what does it mean to be a spokesperson?" I asked.

Vagueness was the response regarding the company. Her question was—would I be interested? Then I got a short tutorial on what a spokesperson might do. Since the company hadn't been identified, as we closed, I told her, "If it's a tobacco or liquor company, I wouldn't be a fit."

A few days later, I received a call from the PR firm for the company. Could I come to New York to meet the marketing team for one of the divisions of Bristol-Myers?

A three-year relationship began that day that included media spokesperson for print, radio, and TV; author of a book; and sponsor of speeches at conferences where women were the predominant attendees.

That led to other spokesperson engagements with different types of companies. Having a sponsor can be a "sweet" deal in a variety of areas. It can involve a daily fee for media appearances; underwriting speeches; underwriting research; purchasing published books to give away; underwriting the publication of a book; underwriting an event … you name it, there are many possibilities.

Sponsorships come in "soft" and "hard" dollars. A radio show, TV station, or podcast may want to feature you, even run an ad for your event. A vendor may want to add some swag to give away to attendees. You don't have to pay for it. That's referred to as a soft sponsorship. Hard dollars deliver moneys toward your expenses— think meeting room rental, printing, audiovisual, food, speaker fees, and other event costs.

Sponsors want "something," It could be a list of attendees with all of their contact information; recognition at your event; an exhibit booth; ads in workbooks; special flyers given to attendees; preferred seating; and your endorsement from the stage or your website. Options are unlimited. For the *Author YOU Extravaganza* I do each year, sponsorship requests go out for bags for all attendees, name badges, breaks, breakfasts, lunches, entertainment, and Wi-Fi for everyone. This all sounds fabulous, doesn't it? If you are interested in the acquisition of a sponsor (or several), there are several elements that you should have in place. Start with the following:

1. **Have a platform in place.** What's your message? Who is it for? What's the size of your community—social media, blog followers, and emails in your database?

2. **Know your ideal target market and its demographics.** What statistics do you have that support the rationale for a sponsor? How big is the market? Where does it spend money? What is the educational level? Gender and cultural?

Income level? What TV shows does it watch? What books does it read?

For example, if women are your market, did you know that 85 percent of women are the primary influencers where money is spent? If your expertise, book, or platform is directed toward women, understand that huge amounts of advertising/marketing moneys are allocated to get their attention.

Resources such as the media have "media kits" for potential advertisers (sponsors). Check websites to determine if they are posted online, or call the main office (radio, TV, newspaper, or magazine) and request one. There is a boatload of demographic information contained in media kits.

3. **You need a written proposal.** It needs data in it. It needs statistics to back up that you fit the target sponsor's demographics.

It needs the "why"—as in why you are the "one." It needs a compelling story—yours or someone you have impacted.

Knowing who to pitch your proposal to is essential. The majority of my sponsorships have come through either the public relations firm, marketing department, or a brand manager of a company. Most likely, yours will be as well. Sponsorships are about relationships. Bypass approaching via social media and email. Phone and voice, and face-to-face is where you start ... along with a killer proposal and then follow-up.

Your proposal needs a dollars-and-sense approach to it. The someone who writes the checks needs to buy into what you can bring to the company. And that "someone" needs to believe that you are worth every dime that sponsor is giving you.

4. **You need to illustrate that you are the "right fit" for the sponsor.** Do it by:

   - telling them what you do and why you do it;

   - including your demographics;

   - revealing what benefits you offer the potential sponsor;

   - promising what you will deliver for them; and

   - letting them know if you have others on your team who advise you.

5. **Don't be shy—ASK for the money.** And don't ask for too little. What's little—anywhere from a few hundred dollars to a few thousand. According to Linda Hollander, expert in training others on how to get sponsors, you should not request less than $10,000 and ideally, propose a one-year commitment. Whatever the amount you want, ask for it.

Sponsorships add to your credibility and enhance your status as an expert, not to mention your cash flow. Sponsors can come from a variety of sources—your target market is your guide. Using target market demographics, look for companies interested in selling their products to your market. Create a template proposal that you can then customize for each company you pitch to. Good luck!

21

Don't Be a Swooper ... the Power of Hanging Out!

You will sell far more books by being present and hanging out.

Delivering an excellent presentation should be the goal of every speaker. Definitely, it's one of the paths to getting repeat and referral business.

So is hanging out ... and schmoozing ... and networking.

When a group hired me, I made it a practice to be at the event for at least the entire day that I was scheduled to speak. Some events may be for a few hours; some a full day; and some multiple days.

- If it was just a few hours, I offered "pick my brain" time after I spoke to attendees or managers/executives.

- If it was a full-day event, I would be there the entire day, making myself available to attendees to ask and get answers to questions they might have.

- If it was a multi-day event, and my schedule allowed it, I would attend the entire conference. Again, being available to meet with attendees was key.

"Why," you might ask.

Simply this: I sold far more books by hanging out, schmoozing, networking, and being present. I had the opportunity to speak with attendees about their issues; their companies; other associations they belonged to that had conferences and brought in speakers. It was part of my marketing strategy. I learned quickly that speakers who were swoopers practiced the kiss of referral death.

The group included me in their activities. I got to know more about them. And I learned about a variety of topics, trends, and things I might never have known had I not been there.

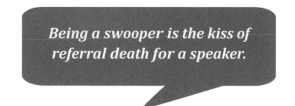

Being a swooper is the kiss of referral death for a speaker.

Because my contract always included a table to offer my educational materials, i.e., books, I always had a designated place to hang out.

Attendees knew where to find me for a chat ... and to buy books.

Swooper speakers usually do a good job from the platform ... but when the talk is over ... they get their check and then head to the door and waiting taxi. The attendees may have thought that the speaker was the cat's meow but—let me tell you—at a conference where there are several speakers, the blur factor can hit. Your presentation melds into the background as stage lights, LCD projector, and microphone are turned on for the next speaker.

My advice: Hang out. You never know who you will meet. My extended time with each group allowed me to learn more about their workplaces when I would join in as a participant in another speaker's breakout. And I definitely sold more books.

If you choose to swoop in, do your thing, and swoop out ... you are making a mistake. Hanging out can create multiple connections with individuals who are connected with or even run other events.

Plus, you sell more books.

Traveling to gigs
can be tiring after
years on the road.
Is it time to bring your
Fans and Followers to you?

22

How to Create a Live Event ... and Why You Should

Creating a Live Event and doing them on an ongoing basis creates Super Fans for you and whatever you are selling and represent. You become an influencer of and a leader in your expertise.

The Why ...

Hot spit ... you have generated a following—
FANS—a tribe of individuals who connect
with you via email or one of your social media
platforms. They look forward to sage advice,
your zany sayings and quotes ... and they want
more. Meaning YOU ... a day or two with just
you ... or maybe you and a few others who
could add to their knowledge base.

The Should ...

Using your expertise to help followers and
followers-to-be is a smart thing to do. Having
face-to-face time with you that an onsite live
event provides; and to experience you and your
wisdom can turn the most casual of followers
into Raving Fans, or what is known among
authors as Super Fans. Super Fans become
your marching marketers—they shout out
through their own social media streams that
you and your products are the best of the best.

The How ...

Are you ready? And if you are game ... where do you start? What are the must-haves that need to be in place? All are good questions. As someone who has created live events for both small and large groups from scratch, it's an ongoing learning experience. I've done my own where it's "just me" and I've done events that have included 20+ speakers. I've done events "in person" using an offsite location ... "at sea" using a cruise ship ... in "my offices" using my outside deck, inner offices or my great room ... and "online" where attendees are a click away. I've done them for a "free admission" and for "paid admission." And I've done events with "exhibitors" ... who pay to be there. In other words, you've got options.

> *Live events are about engagement—with you.*

People like to be connected. Whatever your theme is for the event ... it's where like-minded attendees come together. Make sure you allow for that to happen. Your live event will be about education on your given topic. You've got to figure out how to reach out and connect with prospective attendees; how to continue the connection once they are there; and what you are going to do in follow-up mode.

You need to know your timing—when do you announce the event? If there is a fee, will you have early-bird and late-bird registration fees? What takeaways do you want attendees to embrace? What technology and presentation site will you need? Will it be a water-only event or will you have food? Will you have handouts that need printing or will you supply an online file, leaving it up to each attendee after registration to download?

Live events are about engagement—with you. For online events, there may be engagement if set up ahead of time with attendees and guest speakers. You can create an open mic time for questions or take them via a chat box and respond. For in-person events, schmoozing and networking are a given. At my June three-day *Judith Briles Book Publishing Unplugged* event, I limit the number of participants to less than 50. At the spring and fall *Speaking Unplugged* events, I limit attendance to 25.

Meals and a detailed workbook are included. There are plenty of activities that have attendees moving around and interacting. Authoring and Publishing can be a lonely endeavor—one of my goals for the *Unplugged* event is to seed a community of like-minded authors who desire success.

> *Doing an event has a price tag to it.*

Every live event is different. Some are huge in the number of attendees; where others are small. What's important is to work with a number that you are comfortable with. Some events are designed to get large numbers of attendees in the door—even offering registration for almost nothing. Why would they do that? To get you in the door; the more the better; and they seduce you into buying their products onsite.

Pricing and Costs

Pricing is important. In doing your homework, you need to explore what's "the norm" for your type of event. There could be a range ... but there will be a norm. I would start there and as your demand increases, you can increase your registration fee if you choose.

Doing an event has a price tag to it. It could come at you with hard costs—room rentals; food costs; audiovisual costs; handout costs;

marketing costs; support staff costs; possible transportation costs; even costs to bringing in an outside speaker if that's in your plans. True dollar costs. Then there are "other" costs. Consider your time and, of course, your energy. All costs should be considered when planning event and will directly tie into registration fees. Knowing your "break-even point" for the event is smart business.

Tips to Rock Your Live Event

1. **Start with the topic.** You are the Thought Leader in putting it together. Is it around your expertise ... or is it around others and you are the planner, coordinating speakers and agenda? For me, I always stay with what I know—my expertise—book publishing and working with authors. For my *Judith Briles Book Publishing Unplugged* and *Judith Briles Speaking Unplugged,* it's me. For the *AuthorYOUExtravaganza.org* and

PublishingAtSea.com, I have a team of publishing pros that will deliver workshops dedicated to author, marketing, and publishing success.

2. **Determine how you want to deliver your event.** There are a variety of formats designed for a handful of attendees; a select number or an unlimited number. Some are over the phone; some via a computer; some using YouTube; some via live streaming; and some in person. You may prefer one way or mix them up.

   - **Webinars** can be *info-only, pitch-oriented* for a product or service you offer or a *combo*. Webinars are online events.

   - **Pick My Brain** or **Topic Teleconferences** highlight your expertise and can be *info-only, pitch-oriented* for a product or service you offer or a *combo*. Use one of the "free" conference services to reduce your costs—which is primarily your time in gathering participants.

- Multi-hour public or invitation only **Workshops** can be *info-only, pitch-oriented* for a product or service you offer or a *combo*. They can be online or in-person.

- Multi-day event **Workshops** or **Conferences** can be *info-only, pitch-oriented* for a product or service you offer or a *combo*. They can be online or in-person.

- Weekly or Monthly **Meetups** can be *info-only, pitch-oriented* for a product or service you offer or a *combo*. Setting up a *Meetup.com* group is not complicated; you are the organizer and therefore control the content and "rules" for inclusion (which could include a fee); and Meetup announces the formation of

your group to already existing participants of like-minded members of its
community. New members start to
join. The magnet is the key words you
use to describe what your group is about.

- Facebook Live and Google Hangouts
  can launch you on **Live Streaming**
  and transition to a posting on your
  YouTube channel.

3. **Your initial task is to connect with
   attendees and get them registered.**
   Are they coming from your lists only?
   What about "like" groups on *Meetup.com*?
   Do you have partners/affiliates who will
   be shouting out to their followers, and
   you pay a commission or affiliate fee to
   them if anyone registers through their
   links? Are you going to be doing ads,
   such as on Facebook or Google? Will you
   be doing a special social media campaign
   around it? Or webinars? What about

pushouts on your blog or being featured on a podcast?

How are you going to keep track of registrants—an Excel spread sheet; Eventbrite; using email management tools like aWeber or Mail Chimp; or something else? The names and emails will be an essential part of your future marketing.

Mistakes commonly made are in thinking every presentation has to be all new. You can incorporate information shared previously. Do add new items and rework what you've done with a twist. Remember, re-purposing is your friend.

4. **Don't Underestimate Social Media— it's your Town Hall Shout-Out.** For every event I do, there is a special social media stream of posts for Facebook, Google+, LinkedIn, Twitter, and a Pinterest board.

Blogs are created, plus a special email blast to all within my contact database.

As the early-bird deadline approaches, we use a "countdown" – in 3 days ... in 2 days ... in 1 day ... Final Day to Save Money (or put an actual amount—in my case it was $150). Putting a "clock" on your registration will add to your success and the potential attendees' urgency reflex.

On your Events tab (create one on your website), have a special page with more details, add images that relate to your event and topic. If you have already held one, add quotes from past attendees and images. You should have a "buy" button, and make sure site info for the event is included with a phone number that an interested visitor could call and get more information.

What you want is a wide net. And to assist you, you want some type of a social media management tool, such as Hootsuite, so that you can set up massive postings over a period of time ... and then check it off your to-do list.

5. **Set your budget and determine what you will charge.** Or, you could do a freebie. No matter what, there will be some type of minimal expense. Ideally, you will want to make money. The savvy event-giver will research what others are doing in topic area. If you are the "go-to" expert ... you can set the pricing.

6. **Turn your participants into participants before your Event starts**. A pre-survey can be a gold mine of info for you, including "adds" to your event that you hadn't thought of. Typically, you will post an agenda or bullets of all the items you will explore during your event. Create a "Tell

me about YOU" survey. You can deliver it
as each registers or you can do it in mass,
such as after the early-bird registration
ends or even a few weeks before the big
day. Ask what their goals are and/or why
they are attending. Tools are readily
available for both online poll-taking as
well as an onsite survey that participants
can access via their mobile device.

Companies like *EventMobi.com* create
mobile surveys and polling tools that
you can test on a free trial.

7. **Tap into a sponsor who can underwrite
   some of your costs.** Events cost money.
   Online ones that consist of a teleseminar
   or a webinar are on the low end. Once
   you get away from your office, moneys
   can flow. Site costs, audio tech needs,
   printed material, and food can run into
   the thousands. Your sponsor could already
   be in your circle as a member or a vendor

who supplies product or services for the type of individual you are targeting.

Sponsorship can come in with "soft" and "hard" dollars. A radio show or podcast may want to feature you, even run an ad for your event. A vendor may want to add some swag to give away to attendees. You don't need it, but it's a perk for all. You don't have to pay for it. That's soft. Hard dollars pay for must-haves—moneys toward room, printing, audiovisual, and food costs. Sponsors want "something." It could be a "live" commercial at your event; a booth setup; ads in workbooks, special flyers given to attendees; or a blog about services. The options are unlimited.

8. **Build momentum.** Get the buzz started. Create ongoing blogs, and social media postings. Identify a hashtag that will be unique to you ... and identify top hashtags for your topic to include in posts as you

build up to and during the event. And encourage people who have registered to post out about your upcoming event.

9. **Have fun.** Yes, this is work and when it's over, you could be exhausted. Plan on a treat for yourself.

10. **Make sure you do a post-analysis of your event**—with yourself; with any staff you have; and follow up with your attendees. What worked; what didn't; what changes and/or add-ons are desired for your next event?

You will have emails. Survey them for feedback. If you are doing a registration event or an event that people just showed up—get emails for all; create a customized link using a resource such as *Bit.ly* or TinyURL with your name or a word that the attendees will connect with your event. Encourage them to go to it and receive a bonus or something special. Ask what steps they are going to take since attending your event.

Congratulate yourself!

Live events that you sponsor are usually an evolution in a speaking career. Speaking at a live event that someone else sponsors is the norm. Before you jump in, I would advise you to start small. Groups like *Meetup.com* can be a great gathering source of like-interested people in one topic. Once you have them, all you need is a place to gather. Sometimes, just bringing the coffee or bagels for an AM event is more than enough. For evening, water may do the trick.

23

55 Speaker Takeaways for Pre … At … After Your Gigs

The confident speaker will play them forward to others.

Pre Your Gig:

1. Be good. That means you practice.
2. Be flexible.
3. Build your expertise.
4. Publish a book. If you have one, start on another.
5. ID a current buzz or problem you can associate with your book.
6. ID your market.
7. Drill down in it.
8. Speak to related groups—meeting planners talk ... if you are good, they tell their counterparts.
9. Ask for referrals ... *Who do you know who brings in speakers and that you would be a fit for?*
10. Create a website that has a specific Speaker tab or is exclusively for speaking. See *TheBookShepherd.com.*
11. Start with groups that you are comfortable with.

12. Be curious and learn about the industry. Learn everything you can. Become "one of them."

13. Create one-sheet—bio; pic; topic titles; brief description; benefit to attendee; kudos.

14. If you have a book, offer to give a percentage of sales to the group.

15. Once you book a gig, ID other groups within the state as an "add-on" possibility and contact.

16. Know your market and audience type— don't commit if you are not a fit. Promise me.

17. Customize an Introduction that "matches" each audience.

18. Use the 1-2-3 approach in marketing— email, phone contact, snail mail.

19. Always have a handout with your name, phone, email, and website.

20. Embrace the Rule of 8 ... expect to make eight contact attempts before you get a yes or no.

At Booking:

1. As soon as you book a gig, offer to write an article for their newsletter or magazine.

2. Negotiate as part of your fee an ad in blog, newsletter or magazine.

3. Offer to write a blog or article for the group—don't forget to include that you will be speaking at their event and make sure you include contact information for yourself.

4. Offer to create a survey for the attendees to identify their concerns or other areas—usually the meeting planner provides distribution. Make sure the surveys come to you.

5. Negotiate as part of your fee a book table or exhibit booth as part of your speaking contract.

6. After booking a gig, immediately send a contract, any "how to work with ..." and your introduction.

7. Encourage the organization to raffle copies of your book after your presentation.
8. Ask the meeting planner to pre-buy copies for each attendee. Offer discount for bulk buy.
9. If the group has an auction, offer to contribute your book(s).
10. Offer upfront to donate a percentage of all book sales to the group.

At Your Gig:

1. If you use visuals, make sure there is a cover of book shown on the screen. Warning: If you are making a CE (continuing education) presentation, this may not be allowed—ask.
2. Ask the introducer to mention to the audience that you will be at your book table after your presentation.
3. Carry an extra introduction with you.

4. Arrive EARLY. If you are traveling, it means arrive the day before the gig.

5. Have enough books—they are impulse buys—meaning on the spot.

6. Show/seed your book by reading something from it during presentation.

7. Always pre-sign books, then personalize with name and date when sold—saves time!

8. Give the meeting planner a few copies for giveaways (or you can during talk).

9. Have order forms and information about your book(s) at each attendee's seat.

10. Create bundles—either with discounts for multiple books or sets of books of more than one title.

11. Create an attractive book table display ... you are a "mini-retail store."

12. Books are an impulse buy—make it easy—accept credit cards, checks, cash, even invoice.

13. Create postcards that have your book cover on one side; a few sentences about your speaking on the other with contact info—include with all book purchases.

14. Include a *discounted coupon for your speaking* if booked within the next 60 days—have them at your book table and hand out to all.

15. Don't take the check and run; i.e., a Swooper. Hang out—you will sell more books and if you are good, you will most likely get referrals for gigs.

16. Be present for opening keynote—refer to it when appropriate and if there are any stories, jokes, etc., that mimic yours—delete them from your presentation. They may be your stories, but if you share them in your talk, your audience will assume you copy the copycatter.

17. Stay away from food two hours before you speak. You want your stomach settled.

18. Don't forget a "health break" before you head to the stage.
19. If your event is at a hotel, stay there.
20. If a close friend or a family member is close by, visit them after your event, not before or during. Your job is to be present for your client and your audience. Don't let yourself be pulled away.

After All Gigs:

1. Contact anyone who gave you a card; offer a discount on next gig; use postcards and emails as follow-ups.
2. Send a thank-you in writing.
3. Ask for testimonial (post on your website) and referrals from meeting planner.
4. Never forget: Persistence and follow-up lead to success so don't wait for the phone to ring—EVER.
5. Stay in contact with past clients. I spoke for one client 13 years in a row.

You will add more to these lists as you grow as a speaker. Always keep in the forefront that speaking is a business and needs to be treated as such. As both the CEO and the product, remember that you need care and feeding, so allow for time off to nurture yourself mentally, physically, and intellectually.

Takeaways are usually common-sense ideas or thoughts that either you discovered yourself or were passed down to you from a mentor or someone within your circle.

The confident speaker will play them forward to others. It is a good thing to do.

24

AfterWord:
YOU ... the Speaker!

Your words are powerful. With them,
you create a magic carpet
for your audience.
Transforming the way they
think; delivering new perspectives
and ideas; supplying the "juice"
that inspires and encourages
them; easing the pain that
they may be encountering; and
delighting them so they are glad
they met you and spent time
hearing your insights, wisdom,
and stories.

As a speaker, when you take center stage, you have been given a gift. In turn, you unwrap it in front of the eyes and ears of your audience. To be given this privilege is truly a two-way present—for your audience; for yourself.

Your speaking platform is set with your words and your expertise. It's woven with the visuals of you, of props and images you use, and how you move about a stage. It's reinforced with your listening and being in tune with what your audience's needs are.

Do you realize how powerful you are? What a difference you have the opportunity to make for so many? And what a responsibility; you have to deliver what you promise you will! You are entering a world where the expiration date only exists when you choose to claim it. A world where you can choose where you work and who you work for. A world where you meet an amazing array of people, experience places and environments you hadn't imagined, and

learn about other ideas you never considered.
What an awesome place to be in. Honor it;
embrace it; appreciate it; and grow with it.

Welcome to my world and the Joy of Speaking.
YOU ... the Speaker!

THANK YOU!

Acknowledgments

Meet My Village ...

Some books come to authors over what seems like an eternity; others flow fast once the writing  starts. *How to Create a $1,000,000 Speech* had to happen. In fact, it was long overdue.

The seeding for this book started when I made the decision to create the *Judith Briles Speaking Unplugged* intensive workshop in the fall of 2017 and the workbook I would need to use during the two days. I sat down and just "dumped" out one-liners that I felt were essential for wannabe speakers to know. Then I expanded them to include "must-knows" for those who are focused on being successful and are already on the path. Next, I added my insider tips ... tips and how-tos from speaking on the international platform for 30 years.

By the time I was finished with the workbook (all 120 pages), I knew I was onto "something." I had just created much of the core material that could be morphed into a narrative book, the one that you are reading … and using.

It was completed on the "high seas" … in a balcony cabin on Royal Caribbean's *Oasis of the Seas*. Having just finishing the week-long workshop I do every January under the *PublishingAtSea.com* umbrella, I stayed on the ship for another week. Between the balcony and cabin, I only left them (morning tea was brought to me and refilled multiple times) for a 15-minute break to get a salad and peach or mango iced tea daily. However, I did relish my nightly reward—dinner in one of the specialty restaurants. Six fourteen-hour days created the entire first draft. I was elated to email content to my editor with one hour to spare before departing the ship.

Water and sun are my muses. The week at sea—a week that I only left my cabin a couple of times during the day—was what I call "myopically focused" ... the book was written. Now the fine-tuning would begin with the help of others.

Joining the *AuthorYOU Mini-Guide Series* that consists of *The CrowdFunding Guide for Authors & Writers; How to Avoid 101 Book Publishing Blunders, Bloopers & Boo-Boos; Snappy Sassy Salty: Wise Words for Authors and Writers; The AudioBook Guide for Authors* and *How to Create a $1,000,000 Speech* was an obvious addition. After all, I've done it and have been speaking for my living for three decades. As with the other books in the *AuthorYOU Mini-Guide Series,* the format had to say fun. It's a small book with big ideas and solutions. And to bring this small book to life, my team came together again in the first round of emails.

Thank you to the awesome Nick Zelinger of *NZGraphics.com*. I am fortunate to have an award-winning book and cover designer who is as flexible as Nick is. "Send your files over and I'll get started." Love what he continues to do.

Thank you to my virtual assistant, Leah Dasalla, who took my sheepie guys and made a series of posters and banners to flow throughout the book. *"This has been a fun project. Always challenging. Are you going to do another one like it?"* Yes, we are. It'll be the next in the *AuthorYOU Mini-Guide Series.*

Thank you to Kelly Johnson of *CornerstoneVA.com* and my favorite Geek Girl. Kelly can do just about anything behind the scenes ... and take center stage when need be. *"I love those sheepie guys ... they always make me smile."* As they do me.

Thank you to Don Sidle, the sheepie guy creator and head honcho at *DonSidle.com*. Coming back for a sixth book appearance, the sheep family has had quite a journey. *"I like whimsy and goofy—you inspired me to bring the sheep out!"*

Who would have thought that sheep would become part of my branding and who would have thought of adding a sheepie gal with a bit of bling and eyelashes to the mix? Don did.

Thank you to my first reader and indexer John Maling, who does some of the sentence tweaking—are you sure you want to say it this way? *"There is plenty of great stuff in here ... do you really want to reveal all you know?"* Always helps when your editor likes the book!

Thank you to Peggie Ireland and Barb Wilson, my editors who always catch things my eyes can no longer see and my head knows have already been fixed, and haven't been. *"We love the variety of these books."* Me too—I think I know what the next one is ... then another book topic pops up.

Thank you to Deborah Rapinchuk, my masseuse with magic fingers, who kneads and soothes my tired muscles for a few hours each month to keep me moving. *"Where are all these knots coming from?"* Let me count the ways!

It takes a village to create a book. It takes a village to keep an author going. And, it takes a village to be successful in your book publishing endeavor.

Find yours and take care of it. Mine rocks ... thank you to all.

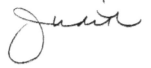

About the Author

Meet Dr. Judith Briles, known as **The Book Shepherd,** Author and Publishing expert, Book Publishing, Crowdfunding, Speaking and Writing Coach, Conference Speaker, Radio Host and the Founder and Chief Visionary Officer of *AuthorYou.org*, a membership organization created for the author who wants to be seriously successful. Publishing and Speaking are in her DNA: She's been speaking since the late '70s, conducting workshops since the '80s and published her first book in 1981. That book was *The Woman's Guide to Financial Savvy* and based on her workshop, Women and Money.

Judith is the author of 36 books—18 published with New York houses until she created Mile High Press in 2000. Based in Colorado, she's published in 16 countries and with over a 1,000,000 copies sold of her work. *How to Create a $1,000,000 Speech* joins *Snappy Sassy Salty: Wise Words for Authors and Writers* and *Author YOU: Creating and Building Your Author and Book Platforms. Author YOU* was selected as a Book of the Year in the Writing|Publishing category at the IndieFab Awards and is considered the must-have workbook for platform building.

Her books have earned over 30 book awards in the Writing|Publishing category from the International Book Awards, Best Book Awards, National Indie Excellence Awards, IPPY Awards, Parents' Choice Awards, IndieFab Awards, Independent Press Award, Book Excellence Award, CIPA Evvy Awards, Colorado Center for the Book Award, and Global eBook Awards. In 2017, Judith was honored to be awarded the first Dan Poynter Legacy Award in Nonfiction. All books in the *AuthorYOU Mini-Guide Series* have earned #1 Best Seller on Amazon.

The *AuthorYOU Mini-Guide Series* launched in 2015 with *The CrowdFunding Guide for Authors & Writers.* In 2016, two additional books were added: *The Author's Guide to AudioBook Creation* by Richard Rieman and *How to Avoid 101 Book Publishing Blunders, Bloopers & Boo-Boos* by Judith. In 2018, *How to Create a $1,000,000 Speech* becomes the latest must-have for authors and writers.

Judith has chaired numerous publishing conferences and is a frequent speaker at writer and publishing conferences. She is the first to tell anyone that her book sales have come through speaking. In her opinion, it's the #1 way to sell books. Each summer, she hosts *Judith Briles Book Publishing Unplugged*, a three-day exclusive "happening" for authors who want to be successful with practical authoring and publishing guidance. In March and November, the *Judith Briles Speaking Unplugged* is delivered with a focus on crafting a speech, developing stories and creating a speaking business.

All information for both Unplugged intensives can be found on her website under the Events tab.

In January, the Publishing at Sea cruise is delivered for the developing and achieving author. Her websites and blogs can be found at *PublishingAtSea.com* and *TheBookShepherd.com.*

Follow @MyBookShepherd and @AuthorU on Twitter and do a "Like" at Judith Briles-The Book Shepherd on Facebook. Join the Author U LinkedIn group and the Author U Google+ community. To book a consult with Judith, you can secure a 30-minute or 60-minute slot at: *http://thebookshepherd.com/pick-judiths-brain.html* or go to her website.

Join 100,000 individuals every month by downloading her podcast, AuthorU-Your Guide to Book Publishing. Access it on iTunes as well as through her website or: *http://bit.ly/BookPublishing-iTunes*

Speaking and Book Shepherding are what Judith does. If you want to create a book that has no regrets, participate in her **Unplugged** events or bring her to your conference, contact her at *Judith@Briles.com.*

When working
with an author,
my goal is to create a book,
a book marketing strategy,
or structure a speech
they proudly present.

How to Work with Judith

Judith Briles
Speaking
Unplugged®
Boot Camp

Dr. Judith Briles is a global speaker who has spoken in 20 countries, all 50 states and created combined speaking fees and book sales totaling $5,000,000 over a 30-year period. In *How to Create a $1,000,000 Speech*, she reveals the ingredients to her secret sauce in how to become a successful speaker.

- Would you like to make $1,000,000 ... and more ... with your mouth and words?
- Would you like to travel to places you never imagined being in ... and meet amazing people?

- Would you like to make a difference in the lives of others ... and get paid to do it?

In the *Judith Briles Speaking Unplugged* two-day intensives you learn by hearing, seeing and experience how to implement her strategies and techniques. Each participant lands in the Hot Seat, where one-on-one coaching is done.

Attendees are talking:

I really enjoyed the 2-day package. Small, intimate setting—the Hot Seats were great. My #1 aha was on how to use a story to lead into my key talk on diversity. Sign me up—I'm coming back!
> —Andi Sue Phillips, author of
> *DeEmphasizing Diversity*

Great job! The first thing I'm going to do is update my current presentation and start using stories that I never considered before. What I learned in the first two hours exceeded my registration fee!
> —Jeannette Seibly, author of *Brag!*

What an amazing depth of actionable information. The material on how to structure contracts and fees will be invaluable. The first thing I'm going to do is refine and define stories. I now know which direction to take.

—Melody Jones, Social Media Expert

The numerous ideas, tips and tricks combined with Judith's amazing expertise will keep me coming back!

—Charles Fischer, author of *Beyond Infinity*

Held twice a year in
Denver, Colorado,
Judith Briles Speaking Unplugged
is limited to 25 participants.

All details are at:
www.TheBookShepherd.com
under the Events tab.

Get ALL the books in Award-Winning AuthorYOU Mini-Guide Series

Designed to give the reader a fast how-to read that delivers essential information and tips on implementation. Learn about the essentials of:

- crowdfunding
- creating an audiobook
- publishing successfully
- becoming a professional speaker
- creating the author platform
- overcoming failure and keeping motivated

Available in Print, eBook, and Audiobook